I0124150

Public Administration and Governance in China

This book aims to explain the gap between Western theories and the Chinese administration reform experiences.

The book provides insights into how the Chinese government can improve its efficiency and legitimacy through reforms and adapt Western theories with Chinese Characteristics. It also looks at the impact of modern technological innovation on reforms and why innovation is a critical key to the political development of China or other countries. The authors also explain how the Internet affects government efficiency.

This timely book is an invaluable reference to better understand the changing theory of global public administration and its practice in developing countries and will interest researchers and policy makers in development studies and public administration and governance.

Leizhen Zang is a Professor at the College of Humanities and Development Studies, China Agricultural University, Beijing. He is also a senior fellow at the Institute of State Governance in Peking University. He was a fellow at Harvard Kennedy School, a Japan Foundation fellow and the JSPS international research fellow at the University of Tokyo. His research covers comparative politics, computational social science methods, and governance.

Yanyan Gao is an Associate Professor at the School of Economics and Management, Southeast University, China. His research interests involve public policy evaluation and the impacts of the infrastructures like High-Speed Rail and Natural Gas Pipeline Projects.

Routledge Focus on Public Governance in Asia

Series Editors:

Hong Liu, *Nanyang Technological University, Singapore*

Wenxuan Yu, *Xiamen University, China*

Focusing on new governance challenges, practices and experiences in and about a globalizing Asia, particularly East Asia and Southeast Asia, this focus series invites upcoming and established researchers all over the world to succinctly and comprehensively discuss important public administration and policy themes such as government administrative reform, public budgeting reform, government crisis management, public–private partnership, science and technology policy, technology-enabled public service delivery, public health and aging, talent management, and anti-corruption across Asian countries. The book series presents compact and concise content under 50,000 words long which has significant theoretical contributions to the governance theory with an Asian perspective and practical implications for administration and policy reform and innovation.

Sustainable Development Goal 3
Health and Well-being of Ageing in Hong Kong
Ben Y. F. Fong and Vincent T. S. Law

Mainland China's Taiwan Policy
From Peaceful Development to Selective Engagement
Xin Qiang

Public Administration and Governance in China
Chinese Insights with Global Perspectives
Leizhen Zang and Yanyan Gao

For more information about this series, please visit www.routledge.com/Routledge-Focus-on-Public-Governance-in-Asia/book-series/RFPGA

Public Administration and Governance in China

Chinese Insights with Global Perspectives

Leizhen Zang and Yanyan Gao

Routledge
Taylor & Francis Group
LONDON AND NEW YORK

First published 2023
by Routledge
4 Park Square, Milton Park, Abingdon, Oxon OX14 4RN

and by Routledge
605 Third Avenue, New York, NY 10158

Routledge is an imprint of the Taylor & Francis Group, an informa business

British Library Cataloguing-in-Publication Data
A catalogue record for this book is available from the British Library

ISBN: 9781032426662 (hbk)
ISBN: 9781032426679 (pbk)
ISBN: 9781003363712 (ebk)

DOI: 10.4324/9781003363712

Typeset in Times New Roman
by codeMantra

Contents

List of figures vii
List of tables ix
Preface xi

1 Understanding Chinese Governance Changes Since 1979: Relationship between the Central and Local Governments 1

2 How Can China Implement Its Policies through Special-Issue-Oriented Governance (SIOG): The Potential Governance Type 29

3 When China's Government Reforms Meet Western Administrative Theories: Do They Fit? 53

4 Political Legitimacy beyond Electoral Democracy: The Crafty Internet Application Strategy in China 73

5 How (When) Does Technological Innovation Improve Government Efficiency? An Empirical Investigation with Cross-National Evidence 97

6 Are Democratic Countries More Efficient in the Public Sector? An Empirical Study with Cross-National Data 126

7 Small Is Beautiful: Fighting Poverty with Low-Input-Technology in China Rural Area 157

Index 161

Figures

1.1	Local financial incomes and expenditures	12
2.1	The frequency of SIOG in the State Council Bulletin	37
2.2	The cycle of SIOG	40
2.3	Model of the effects of matrix governance	42
3.1	The number of CSC, and ASC, and RLSC	61
3.2	The number of jobs posted and the number of civil servants hired in China central government	63
3.3	The simple Analytic Hierarchy Process model	67
4.1	The number of draft laws and draft administrative regulations posted for opinions online (2005–2017)	88
5.1	The proportion of missing data	104
5.2	The relationship between governance efficiency and the country's innovation	106
5.3	Distribution of democracy scores	114
A5.1	The coverage of sample countries	125
6.1	Input-oriented and output-oriented efficiency in a BCC model with one input and one output	130
7.1	Application of low-input-technology in all links of agricultural production	158

Tables

1.1 Overview of China's vertical management departments 8
1.2 The ratio of Chinese government's extra-budgetary fiscal revenue and expenditure in 2002–2010 13
2.1 The frequency of SIOG in CPC documents 36
2.2 The discrepancy between taxpayers and government officials 44
2.3 Characteristics of SIOG and comparison with other types 48
3.1 Different perspectives in different periods 56
3.2 Major institutional reforms in China and international inspiration (theories and practices) 58
3.3 The number of organizations after all previous reforms of the State Council 62
4.1 Differences of China's legitimacy strategies in the Internet era 91
5.1 Descriptive statistics for the status of missing data from the country and year 104
5.2 Descriptive statistics for primary selected variables 105
5.3 Multi-collinearity test 108
5.4 Results of multiple linear regression 110
5.5 Results of fixed effect model 113
5.6 The result of regression analysis of countries with various democracy level 115
5.7 Results of robust test 116
A5.1 The importance degree of variables from random forest 122
A5.2 Collinear relationship of the variables 123
A5.3 Country list 124
6.1 Descriptive statistics 134
6.2 Summary on the scores and rank of public sector efficiency across countries 136

6.3 Democracy and public sector efficiency 139
6.4 Regime durability and public sector efficiency across countries 142
6.5 Institutional quality and public sector efficiency across countries 144
6.6 Institutional quality and regime durability 146
A6.1 Definition of variables and data source 151
A6.2 Efficiency scores and ranks of public expenditure 154

Preface

"Governance" is a ubiquitous but complicated concept. Peer-reviewed publications on governance have grown rapidly since the 1980s. News on governance has also increased on social media and mass media. According to the statistics of China National Knowledge Infrastructure (CNKI) database, there are 4.6 million search results (in Chinese) on "governance", compared with 2.6 million English results in Google Scholar.[1]

Scholars are devoting themselves to governance research with unparalleled enthusiasm. However, there are considerable differences in the understandings of "governance" from the perspectives of individuals or countries. On the one hand, governance includes several secular and universalizing values, such as improving government efficiency and information transparency. On the other hand, different countries also have different contexts. The understandings of governance in developing countries cannot fully imitate the experience of developed countries.

From China's perspective, this book tries to analyze two questions empirically. First, has China's reform experience contributed indigenous paradigms and knowledge to disciplines such as political science and public administration? Second, how can China's administrative reform learn from Western academic theories and experiences in the age of globalization, and how can these theories and experiences affect China's policy-making? From a global perspective, the authors try to explore the general value of government reform. In particular, how micro-technological innovations and macro-systems affect government operations still deserves attention.

This book has seven chapters—Chapter 1 discusses the Chinese governance mechanism based on the relationship between the central and local governments, which provides important clues for exploring the development trend and characteristics of centralization and decentralization.

However, when the government places too much emphasis on Chinese characteristics, such as traditional culture and confidence in the socialist system, it is unwise to use Western theories as a single guideline for reform. Chapter 2 first analyzes different governance types and their influences on China's reform. The authors then analyze the dilemma of different governance types in China practices and the advantages of SIOG (China special-issue-oriented governance). By comparing SIOG with other governance types, the authors highlight the value of governance tools with Chinese characteristics.

Chapter 3 reviews seven national government reforms since China's reform and opening up.

The author analyzes the theoretical support, goals, achievements, and lessons of the reform. The findings reveal a close relationship between China's reform practices and popular Western public administration theories.

Chapter 4 analyzes how the Internet contributes to the legitimacy of authoritarian states, based on four cases from China. The authors divide China's strategy of using the Internet to consolidate legitimacy into four categories, revealing the source of complexity for legitimacy beyond elections.

Chapter 5 focuses on how technological innovation can promote government efficiency. Using panel data from more than 100 countries, the investigation has revealed that the relationship between technological innovation and government efficiency is not a simple linear correlation but a more complicated inverted U-shaped correlation. We also distinguished the impacts of technological innovation on government efficiency in countries with different democratic levels.

Chapter 6 analyzes the political determinants of government efficiency. Based on the comparison of different countries, the authors point out that it is not the level of democracy but the durability of political regimes that could affect government efficiency more. Meanwhile, high levels of economic development and property rights protection, together with a low level of corruption, play fundamental roles in lifting public-sector efficiency by shaping long-lasting political regimes.

Chapter 7 briefly analyzes how the Chinese government deals with poverty. Anti-poverty is one of the sustainable development goals. However, farmers in developing countries generally have poor sci-tech literacy, and it is difficult to master complex modern agricultural technology. Chinese local officials innovatively apply retro-tech (easy-tech), which is easy for farmers to accept, into agricultural production, greatly increasing grain output and helping farmers get rid of poverty.

There are voluminous books on Chinese politics and public administration. We hope this book can encourage those interested in Chinese studies to rethink the new changes in this field. Finally, we have our sincere gratitude to Hong Liu, Wenxuan Yu, and Routledge editors: Yongling Lam, Payal Bharti, and Rajamalar. Their professionalism, devotion to work, and friendliness have given much academic support for this book's writing, modifying, and polishing.

Note

1 See details, https://scholar.google.com and http://www.cnki.net, access date: October 1, 2020.

1 Understanding Chinese Governance Changes Since 1979

Relationship between the Central and Local Governments

1 Introduction

There have been two parallel tendencies of governance in China. On the one hand, the central government is committed to maintaining political unity in a centralized manner; on the other hand, local governments have to adapt to the changing political and economic environment. Coordinating the complex relationship between the central and local governments still has a profound impact on China's current governance structure (Huang, 2008). The local government autonomy has positively impacted national political practice and encouraged numerous scholars to consider China's governance structure from different perspectives. Then, concepts like "consultative authoritarianism" (Zhou et al., , 1993), "decentralized authoritarianism" (Xu, 2011), and "market-preserving federalism" (Weingast, 1995) were proposed to describe the relationship between the central and the local in contemporary China.

With the accumulation of experience in reform and opening up, China's governance achievements and experience need to be further explored in shaping economic development, maintaining political stability and legitimacy, deepening reform of the administrative system, and innovating social governance patterns. To study these issues in depth, researchers not only need to analyze the specific situation but also need to observe the operating mechanism and logic of different systems. At the same time, it is necessary to summarize the subtle interaction between the central and local governments and to grasp the characteristics and connotations of Chinese governance from the perspective of history. Although many scholars try to summarize the laws behind the relationship between the central and local governments, Chinese governance is constantly changing due to its dynamic learning and pilot work, which makes the exploration of China's development model need to be tracked continuously.

DOI: 10.4324/9781003363712-1

Therefore, to discover the political operation mechanism and further understand the governance development since China's reform and opening up, this chapter will study the changing characteristics of the interaction between the central and the local. First, we systematically analyzed traditional research perspectives and theories on this issue. Then the authors make a theoretical analysis of Chinese governance from the perspectives of political power, fiscal power, and public governance. Next, this chapter analyzes the development experience of Chinese governance. It proposes two concepts: governance rectification (timing and boundary of decentralization and centralization) and institutional inclusion (the integration of democracy and centralism). Finally, the authors analyzed and predicted the potential challenges and development trends of China's governance.

2 Understanding China's Governance Changes—Relationship between the Central and Local Governments

China is a country with the largest population, complex geographical conditions, ethnic composition, and social stratum in the world. It is challenging to realize both the unified management of the central government and the coordinated development of local governments. The central government should establish institutional supply arrangements and guidelines that are universal, considerate, and long-term stable according to its own development stage. At the same time, local governments need to propose specific governance measures with regional characteristics and in line with the general trend of local economic development.

Since 1949, political and economic pressures both at home and abroad have continually affected China's development. For example, the Cultural Revolution, the collapse of the former Soviet Union, and radical political shifts of Eastern Europe in the 1980s have threatened China's political stability and weakened Chinese people's political beliefs. However, China's market-oriented reforms, economic growth, and political stability all performed well. Therefore, China's political resilience and adaptability have attracted the attention of scholars. The existing empirical results and theoretical contributions can be interpreted from three aspects.

First, personnel appointments determine the central and local roles in the governance system. Some scholars have pointed out that the central government is the decision-maker and executor of a powerful incentive mechanism. In contrast, local governments face the pressure of performance appraisal, and a temporary interest alliance will be formed among local governments. This may explain why some central policies are difficult to promote and implement locally.

Some scholars have adopted the "tournament system" to describe local governance behavior under the central government's decentralization incentives. They believe that the decentralization of power from the central government has triggered a development competition among local governments. In this competition, the central government that controls the personnel promotion is the judge of regional performance.

Some scholars have also pointed out that the relationship between the central and local governments in China is in a state of "divide and rule", and they believe that the responsibility of the central government for personnel appointment lies in "governing officials". In contrast, local governments focus on "governing the people" in specific areas of affairs. This governance system can disperse the governance risks of the central government, regulate the power of the central government, and ensure the stability of China's political system (Cao, 2011).

Other scholars have described China's government structure and operation mode of administration as the "administrative contracting system," suggesting that the central government is essentially a business contractor. It subcontracts economic development, public services, and social security to local governments, and uses fiscal transfer payments and personnel appointments to ensure the effectiveness of central power and local governance (Zhou, 2016).

Second, fiscal power is the driving engine for the central and local in the economic field. Scholars have proposed that China's operation of political power before the reform and opening up features "overall dominance," that is, the central government makes an overall arrangement of local fiscal revenues and policies. However, after the reform and opening up, the power structure turned to specialization and precise division of labor, which made the arrangement of central–local relations and national governance more reasonable (Feizhou & Xing, 2009).

Some scholars have adopted "soft authoritarianism" and "decentralized authoritarianism" to describe China's fiscal decentralization strategy, arguing that this form of power division helps to stimulate the locals to contribute more to economic development. This driving force of economic growth is an essential mechanism for forming the "Chinese model" (Fukuyama, 1992; Landry, 2008). Scholars have also proposed "fragmented authoritarianism," arguing that although the political system is under the unified control of the central government, the decision-making power is distributed to government departments of different levels and functions, making it possible for local governments to bargain, especially on the allocation of fiscal powers (Lieberthal & Oksenberg, 1990; N. Lu, 2018).

Third, the administrative authority is the basis for the central and local decentralization in public governance. The piloting and promotion of policies are distinct mechanisms formed in China's long-term practice. They have become the main interactions between the central and the local since China's reform and opening up. With diversified forms of policy piloting, scholars have conducted further observations and explorations on the central–local relationship and found that distribution of administrative authority is key to the effectiveness of local governance, which has contributed many theories to improving China's public policies. And, the concept of "hierarchical experimentation" summed up by German scholar Sebastian Heilmann has revealed that China's point-to-surface process of policy exploration explained the decentralization rules of public governance authorities more systematically, specifically, and made a practical interpretation to the integration of local innovation spirit and central dominant position (Heilmann, 2008a).

It can be seen that a complex theoretical system has been initially formed based on China's central-local relationship. The divergence and complementation between concepts have enriched China's governance and laid a foundation for predicting the future directions of governance. However, most existing research was derived from observation and textual research on a single phenomenon, lacking comparative analyses between theoretical systems. To make matters worse, the pursuit of simplicity and universality of concepts makes some theories less stable when interpreted. A direct copy of Western values and the lack of localization make it difficult for the theoretical interpretation of China's governance to effectively shift the paradigm and innovate, thus presenting the disorder.

The existing research generally fails to clarify the combining features of decentralization and centralization, the timing and boundary of decentralization and centralization, and the value norms in China's governance mechanism.

Moreover, China's governance development showed different characteristics at different stages, which determines that the interpretation of governance mechanisms needs to begin with various fields and calls for comparative analysis from a diachronic perspective. To make up for shortcomings of the researches as mentioned above, in this chapter, we combine macro-historical evolution with micro-case analysis and adopt views of political power, economic power, and public governance to interpret the characteristics of China's governance in the context of central-local relationship changes in details.

3 Stylized Facts of China's Governance Development—Interactive Changes in the Central-Local Relationship

Although there are natural hierarchical hedges between China's central and local governments, and their governance objectives are pretty different, a flexible power structure always allows the two to find a balancing point, which is a process to turn the country's general goals into specific actions. During this transition process, the external environment and response continue to influence the governance structure of the government. Any shift or reform in (ideological) direction heralds a shift in political, economic, and public governance power. This also facilitates discussions on central-local interactions and evolutionary processes. Therefore, following discussion will be divided into three aspects.

3.1 Combination of Centralization and Moderate Decentralization of Political Power

Since 1949, the power to appoint and remove important leading cadres has been strictly controlled by the central government. This restraint of power is also seen as a safeguard for China's unified state structure. In reality, however, the central government's control over the appointment and removal of local leaders is not static. This is closely related to the market-oriented reform process. Specifically, after the reform and opening up, the changes in the central and local personnel appointment rights have roughly gone through three stages.

In the first stage, the power to appoint personnel is highly controlled by the central government. Before 1983, the central government implemented a system of "supervising two lower levels," the central government directly investigated, appointed, and dismissed leaders at the provincial, ministerial, and departmental levels. However, the rapid increase in the number of officials will put great pressure on the central government's human resources management, and it will also not help local governments to make effective decisions. Therefore, this has led to a series of bureaucratic malpractices such as administrative rigidity and red tape. On the one hand, in the early stage after the country's founding, the bureaucratic system and cadre team building was deficient. It required direct leadership and arrangement from the central government. On the other hand, in the early stage of reform and opening up, the central government needed to restore the party and government cadres damaged by the Cultural Revolution. A large-scale and direct personnel management system was adopted. Based on this, China's governments at all levels were able to recover quickly from the disordered political movement, re-establish the state political authority, and ensure its unity of top-down governance.

In the second stage, the power of appointment and dismissal was moderately decentralized. With the improvement of the administrative system at all levels and clarification of functions, and the guiding role of market-oriented reforms in ideological emancipation, the governance autonomy of local governments and the stability of bureaucratic operations increasingly became the basis for effective governance. Therefore, based on the central government's continuous decentralization of economic power, part of the personnel power was gradually delegated to the locals. The landmark event occurred in 1983, with the issuance of *Provisions of the Organization Department of the CPC Central Committee on the Reform of the Cadre Management System*, which made a "little, flexible and fine management" as the guidance of the current political system reform, and limited central personnel power above (at) provincial level. Then in 1984, *Notice of the Organization Department of the CPC Central Committee on Revising the Title List of Cadres under the Management of the CPC Central Committee* was issued. It was clarified that the personnel system of "supervising two lower levels" was revised to "supervising one lower level and registering the other," which reduced the number of leading cadres directly managed by the central government from 15,000 to 3,000. It also led to the decentralization of personnel appointments and the dismissal of the midlevel party and government organizations and delegated them to provincial units. During the same period, the Central Committee discussed and approved the *General Plan for the Reform of Political System* in the Seventh Plenary Session of the Twelfth Central Committee, and proposed the idea of separation of the party and government, decentralization of power, and streamlining of institutions, which further promoted the moderate decentralization of the power on personnel changes.

In the third stage, the operation of power once again embodied the centralization of the power to appoint and dismiss personnel. The decentralization of the central government has stimulated the enthusiasm of local governments, but it has also given local leadership the opportunity to breed sectarianism and local protectionism. Especially in the early 1990s, the people's congresses in some regions even rejected the candidates appointed by the central government and chose local people as leading cadres. This resistance to central personnel management made the central government think about how to strengthen political centralization. Therefore, in 1999, the Central Organization Department issued the *Regulations on Rotations of Cadres*, clarifying that the selection and appointment of local leaders need to comply with non-local principles and implement regular exchanges and rotations. The most evident cases were at the provincial level. For example, chief officials and cadres at provincial and ministerial levels were transferred from other provinces or the central government. The term of office was constantly shortened, and rotation of the incumbents was accelerated. As far as city- and county-level leading cadres were concerned, their personnel turnover had become very frequent. However, when examining the direction and scope of personnel changes, there were fewer personnel changes across administrative regions but more intra-department or inter-department ones within the same administrative area.

To some extent, that left space for the stability of local leading cadres (Barnett, 1967; Walder, 1989). In addition, to achieve the dual goals of reducing the pressure of personnel management and effectively restricting local leading cadres, the central government accelerated the establishment and improvement of the vertical management system since 1994. Then a systematic, centralized system was developed, as shown in Table 1.1. With an increasing number of "government functional departments" and continuous expansion of functional regions involved, local governments' administrative management power and their power of making personnel changes were restricted. Still, strengthening the unity of responsibilities between the central and the local became the bottleneck of the administrative system reform. There is no good way to rationalize the relationship between government functional departments and regions and strengthen political control. However, only by solving this problem, can China's political system design be optimized.

The legislative power is also essential for the interaction between the central and local governments. It also contains centralization and moderate decentralization. Before 1979, the central government has always exclusively owned the power of enacting laws and regulations throughout the country with a strong sense of centralization. However, since the promulgation of "*the Organization Law of Local People' s Congress and Local People' s Government at Various Levels*" in 1979, the provincial governments have obtained independent legislative power on condition that it cannot contradict the country's programmatic texts such as the Constitution, laws, regulations, and

Table 1.1 Overview of China's vertical management departments

Central departments (中央部门)	*Vertical management departments (垂直管理机构)*	*Numbers*
General Administration of Customs (海关总署)	Direct Affiliated Customs (直属海关)	42
Ministry of Water Resources (水利部)	Water Conservancy Commissions (流域水利委员会)	7
State Tobacco Monopoly Administration (国家烟草专卖局)	Provincial Tobacco Monopoly Administrations (省级烟草专卖局)	33
State Post Bureau (国家邮政局)	省级邮政局 Provincial Post Bureaus (省级邮政局)	31
National Audit Office (国家审计署)	驻地方特派员办事处 Resident Offices of China National Audit Office (驻地方特派员办事处)	18
State Forestry Administration (国家林业局)	Resident Offices of State Forestry Administration (地区森林资源监督专员办事处)	14
State Administration of Taxation (国家税务总局)	Provincial Administrations of Taxation (省级国家税务局)	36
Foreign Exchange Administration of the People's Bank of China (中国人民银行外汇管理局)	Provincial Branches of Foreign Exchange Administration of the People's Bank of China (省级分局)	36
China Meteorological Administration (中国气象局)	Provincial Meteorological Administrations (省级气象局)	36
Ministry of Finance (财政部)	驻省级财政监察专员办事处 Provincial Offices of the Ministry of Finance (驻省级财政监察专员办事处)	35
China Seismological Bureau (中国地震局)	省级地震局 Provincial Seismological Bureaus (省级地震局)	31
China Insurance Regulatory Commission (保监会)	Local Regulatory Administrations of China Insurance Regulatory Commission(地方监管局)	36
State Oceanic Administration (国家海洋局)	Branches of State Oceanic Administration (海区分局)	3
Maritime Safety Administration (海事局)	Direct Affiliated Maritime Safety Administrations (直属海事局)	20
China Securities Regulatory Commission (证监会)	Provincial Regulatory Administrations of China Securities Regulatory Commission (省级监管局)	36
People's Bank of China (中国人民银行)	Regional Branches of People's Bank of China (地区分行)	11

Central departments (中央部门)	*Vertical management departments (垂直管理机构)*	*Numbers*
Exit and Entry Administration Bureau (出入境管理局)	出入境边防检查总站 General Stations of Exit and Entry Frontier Inspection (出入境边防检查总站)	9
General Administration of Quality Supervision, Inspection, and Quarantine of the People's Republic of China (国家质检总局)	Provincial Administrations of General Administration of Quality Supervision, Inspection and Quarantine of the People's Republic of China (省级检疫局)	35
Ministry of Industry and Information Technology (工信部)	Provincial Communications Administrations (省级通信管理局)	30
Ministry of Transport (交通部)	Administrations of Basin Navigational Affairs of Ministry of Transport (流域航务管理局)	2
Civil Aviation Administration of China (民航局)	Regional Administrations of Civil Aviation Administration of China (地区管理局)	7
China Banking Regulatory Commission (银监会)	Provincial Regulatory Administrations of China Banking Regulatory Commission (省级监管局)	36
Ministry of Commerce (商务部)	Resident offices of Ministry of Commerce (驻地方特派员办事处)	16
National Bureau of Statistics (国家统计局)	Provincial Survey Offices (省级调查总队)	32
Ministry of Land and Resources (国土资源部)	State Land Supervision Administrations (国家土地督察局)	9
Ministry of Environmental Protection (环境保护部)	Regional Supervision Centers of Environmental Protection (区域环保督查中心)	6
State Administration of Coal Mine Safety (国家煤矿安全监察局)	Provincial Administrations of Coal Mine Safety (省级煤矿安全监察局)	27
National Energy Administration (国家能源局)	Regional Energy Regulatory Administrations (区域监管局)	6
State Railway Administration (国家铁路局)	Regional Railway Regulatory Administrations (地区铁路监管局)	7

Note: The authors collected data from the Central People's Government website of the PRC in 2016.

policies. Then, in the 1980s, the Standing Committee of the National People's Congress made adjustments to the bill, extending the legislative power to provincial capital cities and larger cities approved by the State Council. And the central government readjusted the legislative relationship between the main and the local in the revision of "*the Legislative Law*" in 2015 to allow further the "cities with sub-districts" to obtain their legislative power. Although the legislative power has been decentralized since the reform and opening up, the central government has the power to revoke local laws and regulations. The central government maintains its jurisdiction at the macro-level. The centralization is intended to ensure the central government's highest control over political discourse and prevent the destruction of unity due to excessive local autonomy. At the same time, the decentralization is to coordinate the local development with the overall pace of national economic construction and to provide limited but orderly political incentives for the locals. Political stability and governance unity are not the only factors affecting the central government's political power distribution. Changes in economic development are also the fundamental reason for the imbalance between the central and local power structures. Therefore, it is necessary to conduct a detailed analysis of the relationship between the central and the local from the perspective of fiscal power.

3.2 The Combination of Fiscal Decentralization and Moderate Centralization

Although there are some similarities between central-local relations in the economic field and central-local relations in the political field, the focus is different, for example, in the economic field, China prioritizes decentralization, while politics is the opposite. China has formed a combination of fiscal decentralization and moderate centralization. In general, after the reform and opening up, the central and local financial power interaction took the reform of the tax-sharing system as a turning point and went through two phases.

From 1980 to 1993, the first phase was characterized by the gradual decentralization in fiscal power. Before the reform and opening up, the central government's approach to local financial management changed from "unified state control over income and expenditure" to "unified leadership and hierarchical management." The central government realized that the first pattern had severely restricted the development of local governments and state-owned enterprises (SOEs). Therefore, it granted economic management power to them in 1951 by sharing the aggregate amount of income and dividing fiscal levels. The governance method of unbalanced income and expenditure still could not improve the fiscal subjectivity of local governments or SOEs (Bingyang & Qingwang, 2012), which is why China's planned economy became increasingly rigid.

Therefore, in order to rapidly promote the country's economic growth, the central government has implemented a new fiscal system for classified contracting between the central and local governments since 1980. Different levels of government have formulated a series of fiscal and tax decentralization measures to clarify their respective income items and expenditure fields, and gradually realized the transition to independent financial entities. Under the enlightenment of this fiscal decentralization system, local governments are actively exploring diversified economic growth methods. Moreover, the reform of "collecting taxes instead of profits" carried out by the central government in 1985 greatly stimulated the creativity and initiative of the locals.

The second phase was from 1994 to the present, with the overall trend of the central government moderately controlling and optimally distributing the fiscal power. The relatively radical fiscal decentralization has accelerated economic development, but it has primarily broken the regional equilibrium pattern of economic growth. Concerning the budgetary system of "the division of revenue and expenditure between the central and local governments and classified contract," it is stipulated that regions where fixed income is more than expenditure should turn over quota amount to the central government. In contrast, areas, where fixed income is less than expenditure, should be granted the central government's shared income or special subsidies.

However, some southeast coastal provinces and open cities chose to reduce the local taxation scale to reduce the central government's amount. As a result, the central government's proportion of budget revenue dropped to less than 20% in the 1990s, making it difficult to maintain the transfer payment to economically backward areas. During the same period, the enthusiasm for infrastructure investment in some regions was difficult to suppress, leading to persistently high inflation rates, increasing pressure on people's livelihood, and weakening of political and social stability. The central government implemented the tax distribution system in 1994. Value-added tax is the main body, and consumption tax and business tax are supplemented. National tax revenue is divided into three parts: central government tax, local government tax, and shared tax. In addition to this system, state and local tax bureaus have also been established.

The tax-sharing system is a symbol of centralization, and local governments are responsible for various fiscal expenditures in governance. Judging from the division of central and local tax rates in this system, there is a tendency to maintain a balance of power between the central and local budgets. The remaining tax income regulates the regional budget regarding the central government's fiscal expenditure and national defense and foreign affairs. The central government can achieve macroscopic control through a tax refund, transfer payment, and project operation. In general, though the reform of the tax distribution system has shaped a 50–50 pattern regarding central-local fiscal income (see Figure 1.1), local governments' budgetary power still cannot match their responsibilities. Developed regions turn over substantial taxes, whereas under-developed areas lack economic development motivation, causing significant differences in China's regional development levels and governance capabilities.

Although the tax-sharing system maintains the central government's ability to control the economy, local governance still needs full financial autonomy in the era of market economy. Revenue cannot cover local budget expenditures. Therefore, in order to balance the budgetary power of the central and local governments, the central government gives the right to grant land, highlighting the second feature of this phase—optimizing distribution. As early as 1999, the Ministry of Land and Resources issued the "*Notice on Further Implementing the Bidding and Auctioning of the Use of State-Owned Land*." Local governments have successively changed the development mode into "bidding, auctioning and listing." Moreover, the "*Regulations on the Transfer of State-owned Land Use Rights by Bidding, Auction and*

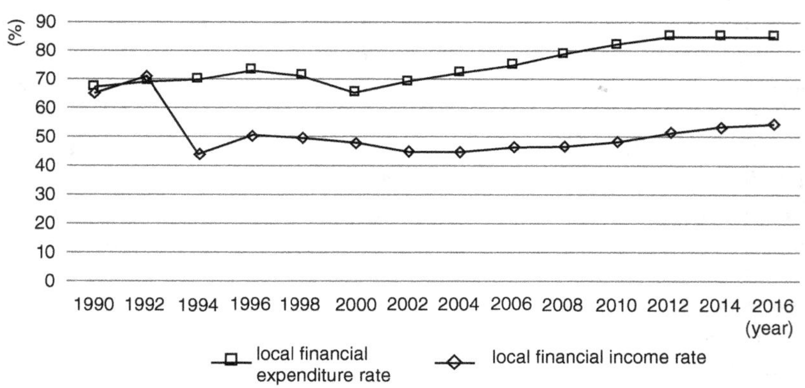

Figure 1.1 Local financial incomes and expenditures

Listing" promulgated by the Ministry of Resources in 2002 further regulated the procedures and scope of local land finance, alleviating the local governments' fiscal pressure.

The local government transformed state-owned land into industrial areas, commercial areas, residential areas, medical areas, and education areas, which greatly increased the local government's extra-budgetary revenue (as shown in Table 1.2), which not only alleviated the pressure on fiscal expenditure but also promoted China's urbanization, industrial innovation, and employment rate. In this context, some researchers have found three dimensions of interaction between the central and the local, and that among the local governments.

First, the central government's collection of fiscal power has stimulated the locals to sell land to expand income. Second, faced with promotion pressure, local governments have started land financial competition. Third, different periods of leaders and cadres in the same position have adopted differentiated land development strategies to create new performance growth points.

This kind of competitive land management contributed significantly to performance growth in the short term. However, the local government's over-reliance on land has also caused the over-utilization of resources and the malformation of urban development. The huge amount of compensation for demolition and relocation by local governments has exposed the shortcomings of land finance.

Table 1.2 The ratio of Chinese government's extra-budgetary fiscal revenue and expenditure in 2002–2010

Year	*Extra-budgetary fiscal revenue (100 million yuan)*		*Extra-budgetary fiscal expenditure (100 million yuan)*		*Local revenue ratio (%)*	*Local expenditure ratio (%)*
	Central	*Local*	*Central*	*Local*		
2002	440.00	4,039.00	259.00	3,572.00	90.18	93.20
2003	379.37	4,187.43	329.32	3,827.04	91.69	92.08
2004	350.69	4,348.49	389.50	3,962.23	92.54	91.05
2005	402.58	5,141.58	458.34	4,784.14	92.74	91.26
2006	467.11	5,940.77	377.72	5,489.23	92.71	93.56
2007	530.37	6,289.95	453.34	5,659.08	92.22	92.58
2008	492.09	6,125.16	402.13	5,944.23	92.56	93.66
2009	352.01	6,062.64	459.20	5,769.09	94.51	92.63
2010	399.31	5,395.11	386.37	5,368.32	93.11	93.29

Source: Statistical Yearbook of China (2003–2011).

In conclusion, China's central-local relationship in the economic field is generally in a state of decentralization. Local fiscal decentralization is the typical result of China's market-oriented reform and the complexity of authorities. Moreover, it manifests that the effectiveness of local governance plays a supporting role in national development. Meanwhile, moderate centralization also reflects that economic growth needs to be compatible with the balanced development of the country and the healthy transformation of society. Therefore, instead of federalism, China's fiscal system is a dynamic centralization and decentralization with high flexibility.

3.3 The Combination of Top-Level Design and Local Self-Governance

From the interactive central-local relationship in the political and economic fields, it can be seen that the Chinese governance behaviors have become more diversified since the reform and opening up. This provides a favorable condition for social transformation and democratic development. However, since the long-term governance goal is to maximize economic growth, local governments focus too much on the market and neglect social development. Consequently, the complexity of the social structure has exacerbated the incoordination and inadequacy of social construction (Bardhan, 2002).

Efficient public administration is an indispensable driving force for social development. Local governments shoulder important political tasks such as social stability and economic development (X. Lu, 2012). Therefore, it is necessary for us to fully understand China's governance mechanism, and to introduce China's central-local relations research into the field of public administration.

The idea of "pilot first and then promote" has been explored by CPC as early as in the revolutionary war. After the reform and opening up, this typical pilot governance behavior was adopted more frequently. It promoted the administrative system's top-down reforms and played a vital role in social policy areas, such as education, medical services, social security, environmental protection, and governmental reaction. This chapter analyzes the interaction characteristics and laws of the central and local public administration. The following three aspects will be elaborated.

First, the central-dominated top-level design does not exclude local self-governance behavior. Regarding China's pilot governance, many scholars have focused on top-down approach. That is to say, the central government put forward policy objectives or determine policy tools and then authorize some local governments to conduct the pilot reform first. Some Western scholars refer to this type of governance as "adaptive governance" (Heilmann & Perry, 2011) or "classified pilot" (Heilmann, 2008b), symbolizing the governance mode of centralization of decision-making power. However, the central governance objectives are not always applicable. The top-level approach only provides the local with governance directions and principles. In contrast, the local's specific governance tools and strategies still need to be explored, thus forming the co-existence of top-level design and local independent decision-making.

Second, local self-governance can promote the implementation and improvement of top-level design. Local government-dominated self-exploration, in addition to design experiments, is also the entry point for many scholars to study Chinese experimentalism, which encourages local creation and self-practice without authorization. According to this mechanism, the center's function is to inspect where the governance reform is innovative and achieved particular accomplishments and to learn and promote the local governance experience nationwide.

For example, China's rural social pension insurance system was initiated in the early 1990s. Still, due to inflation and constantly falling interest rates of bank deposits, the old-style personal contribution system could not meet the needs of old-age care for rural residents. Therefore, after 1999, local governments began to explore and implement new ways actively, striving to put forward a more effective and feasible rural pension insurance system. In 2006, Baoji, Shaanxi Province introduced a pension system that combined individual contributions, rural collective subsidies, and government financial subsidies, increasing farmers' access to pensions and alleviating government expenditure pressure. Baoji was chosen as a pilot city for rural pension insurance system reform by the Ministry of Human Resources and Social Security in 2007. In 2012, the experience and practice were promoted nationwide. With self-innovation first and pilot selection second, this kind of governance practice was known as the "recognition" pilot trigger mechanism, which is more feasible and stable than a top-down innovation pilot. Despite the absence of central authorization and policy support, the achievements of this governance pilot are still superior.

Third, the learning mechanism among local governments provided a link between top-level design and self-governance. Policy diffusion, including top-down policy promotion, horizontal competition among local governments, and bottom-up policy learning, is a critical way to promote the formation of better national policies (Xufeng & Hui, 2018). The spontaneous policy learning provided space for local governments to conduct non-competitive interactions and increased the possibility of transitioning from local governance experience to top-level design. Taking the example of the building of the Internet petition system, the State Council advocated the establishment of a petition information system nationwide in 2005. It proposed that all localities should open online petition channels in 2007. However, the lack of clear policy instructions and expected goals enabled the locals to carry out exploration extensively. Thus, Huai'an, Jiangsu Province, established a "Sunshine Letters and Visits" information system, which was acknowledged and adopted by many cities. In 2004, it was recognized by the National Public Complaints and Proposals Administration as a model and called for the nationwide promotion of Huai'an's experience.

Indeed, policy learning among local governments has always been accompanied by policy reproduction. That is to say: policy learners usually do not indiscriminately copy initial policy. Instead, they selectively absorb and modify them, which may cause a deviation from policy effect.

The central government does not always show a laissez-faire attitude toward local learning. On the contrary, it will use the top-level design to guide the learning process.

In general, the complex mechanism of public administration in China allows local governments to maintain daily operations and achieve effective governance. Moreover, it is also a channel for the central government to plan national development and deepen administrative reforms. In the modern era of mutual consultation and governance, the combination of top-level design and self-governance provides an excellent opportunity to break through the bureaucratic barriers.

4 The Experience of China's Governance Development

Many characteristics of Chinese governance can be seen from the respective roles of the central and local governments in public management and power distribution. The central government is shifting from centralized control to local governments to give full play to their enthusiasm. Resource conditions and political preferences in different regions lead to diverse power distribution and governance characteristics.

In terms of personnel organization, financial operations, and public management, centralization and decentralization coexist, reflecting the flexible thinking of governance at all levels. Though the development of China's governance showed complexity and volatility, there are still lessons to learn. Some scholars have used concepts of "co-governance of the central and local governments" "monitoring ability of governance performance and balance of residual distribution rights" to describe China's governance patterns. They have contributed a lot to summarizing and refining the Chinese governance model.

However, from the perspective of dynamic equilibrium, the centralization and decentralization of different powers have common characteristics in governance objectives and dynamic mechanisms. And, China's governance mechanism is reflected in power shifts and democratization, and decentralization in terms of governance.

4.1 Governance Rectification: Timing and Boundary of Decentralization and Centralization

It can be seen from the development of China's governance that the coexistence of decentralization and centralization is an essential feature of the central-local interaction. Decentralization can help reduce the central government's risk in governance, stimulate the local governments' enthusiasm for development, and improve the rationality of national decisions. Centralization can promote the stability of political operations, avoid market economic risks, and optimize resource allocation. Although the characteristics mentioned earlier guide understanding China's governance mechanism, they can only explain the purpose and motivation of power distribution, not its timing and boundary, which is key to understanding the essence of institutional adjustments in China. After re-examining China's practice of centralization and decentralization in various fields, we can see that governance failure or deviation is often the turning point for power structure changes. The following part will further analyze China's governance experience from this perspective.

There are many governance deviations, which can often be concluded as failed efforts to meet designated goals. At the same time, a flexible transformation between decentralization and centralization is a vital way to realize governance rectification. China's governance system itself is a contradiction-complex: on the one hand, few countries and regions can compare with China in terms of governance tasks and governance difficulty. After decades of war and the cultural revolution, China could not quickly shake off its backwardness. However, China is also the backbone of communist countries and a leading developing country. Therefore, its strong sense of development and competition is transformed into strong pressure on governance performance. The Communist Party emphasizes its responsibility to develop the country and society.

On the other hand, the tradition of centralization has made governance in all fields depend on the central government's guidance. Different regions have different development foundations and political backgrounds, and macro-governance policies need to be formulated according to local conditions, but it is difficult for the central government to effectively supervise the governance details of each region. Therefore, there is a profound contradiction between centralization and local governance.

Under the constraints of multiple contradictions, absolute centralization or decentralization cannot prevent governance deviation from occurring. For example, the political centralization of the power of appointment and dismissal weakens the autonomy of local governments, and improper decentralization of power leads to regional protectionism. The centralization of fiscal power has weakened the enthusiasm of local governments for development, while fiscal decentralization has seriously affected the central government's fiscal revenue.

In public administration, the centralization of governance authority makes it hard for local governments to implement decisions adaptively. Still, the lack of centralized guidance makes it easy for local governments to fall into the predicament of wasting resources. Although combining centralization and decentralization cannot eradicate governance deviations, a timely transformation between the two can temporarily eliminate the adverse effects of governance failures when deviation occurs. Centralization can help maintain high-level political stability, and appropriate decentralization can also help ensure the stability of local governance. In the context of large-scale decentralization of fiscal power by local governments, the central government has also achieved fiscal transfers to underdeveloped regions through moderate centralization. Public management emphasizes the importance of top-level design, but decentralized local autonomy pilots also provide the central government with valuable reform experience.

Due to the diversity and uncertainty of governance deviations, the transformation of power structure has also been flexible in developing China's governance, and some scholars adopted "contingent decision-making" to describe this feature. However, another question worth pondering is why China's governance mechanism can withstand repeated changes in power structure instead of falling into collapse or rigidity. We believe that the governance goal of "being both certain and ambiguous" is key to shaping the resilience and flexibility of China's governance.

First of all, China's governance goals are very stable. Regardless of changes in the country's political system and economic condition, political legitimacy for officials is fundamental to running and survival. The particularity of the state is manifested in different sources of legitimacy. As far as China is concerned, government performance has always been an essential basis for legitimacy. Financial performance has always been the most important basis for legitimacy in China (Shambaugh, 2001). Therefore, improving economic performance always means development, which is both a central governance goal and a local political task. The bureaucratic championship system theory reveals the relationship between economic development and the promotion of local officials.

At the same time, some scholars have pointed out that the central government's management of local governments is out of date. As long as local governments do not make major mistakes in decision-making or cause widespread dissatisfaction, the central government will secretly endow them with certain governance powers. These all show that the distribution of power is in harmony with the steady development of the locals. Therefore, to ensure that the center has sufficient political control over the local, decentralization and centralization are tools for promoting growth. Hence, personnel appointment and dismissal, fiscal power, and authority can be constantly adjusted between concentration and decentralization.

Then, China's governance goals are also pretty ambiguous. Although the governance aims to promote development at the macro-level, how to achieve development is not clear enough. Under this context, the flexible transformation of power structure becomes a way to resolve the problem of ambiguous governance. The authors think that there are two reasons for the unclear governance objectives at the macro level. On the one hand, the long-term mismatch of authorities and fiscal powers between the central and the local often puts the implementation of national policies into a dilemma with the absence, offside, or misplacement of power, so the central cannot formulate a particular and feasible governance goal.

On the other hand, the central government must bear huge risks in choosing the direction of macro-governance. The central government usually conveys ambiguous political orders such as the conference spirit, reform direction, and overall objective to avoid centralized governance risks. Therefore, the locals must consider their resource conditions and then divide and embody the political signals. In the process of shifting ambiguous political orders to the regularized bureaucratic system, the self-governance ability of local leaders seems to be necessary. To motivate the enthusiasm of the local governments, political decentralization, fiscal decentralization, and governance innovation are needed.

Meanwhile, the local has to put forward clear governance goals. Of course, decentralization may also lead to ambiguous governance. The interception of financial resources by governments at all levels, policy distortions caused by localism, and incontinence in governance innovation will all make governance goals less certain. From in-depth studies of "campaign-oriented governance" and "special governance" in recent years, the daily operation of local governments' bureaucratic system is often affected by the campaign-oriented governance from the central government. The "government functional departments" from "administration power of different departments and regions" became the central agent in this period. It achieved closer-linked governance in the "regions," bypassing and implementing the government orders step by step and then realizing a particular governance objective based on reshaping the authority of central governance (Zang & Zhang, 2019).

In summary, there is no fixed model or power structure in China's governance, and they are always in the process of development. Therefore, centralization and decentralization can be continuously tried and flexibly transformed as the primary form of interaction between the central and the local. Both of them regard development as the motivation and objective of governance; the governance deviation becomes the timing and boundary of the centralization and decentralization. At the same time, as a specific and vague governance objective, pursuing development and how to achieve development have created space for centralization and decentralization, which also gave birth to China's flexible and resilient governance mechanism.

4.2 Inclusive System: The Value Combination of Democracy and Centralization

Talcott Parsons (2010) has argued that ruling politics based on empiricism is not the foundation to establish a state and that value norms are the reasons for a state's legitimacy. Decentralization and centralization are only the essential characteristics of central-local interaction and governance mechanisms. The combination of democracy and centralization is the governance value and norm that maintains the balance of central–local relations. Though democracy and concentration are generally defined as the fundamental organizing principle of the Chinese Communist Party, it has been deeply integrated into various fields of state governance, becoming another characteristic of China's governance mechanism.

First, the governance mechanism is viewed from a democratic perspective. Democracy in China tries to reach consensus through political consultation. It advocates that political elites and the public participate in the political process together, seek a balance of interests with mutual understanding and dynamic feedback, and form a "governable democracy" oriented by public values. Democratic centralism is a vivid embodiment of consensus democracy. Under the guidance of democratic principles, party members have the right and obligation to make suggestions for the development of the organization. At the same time, significant issues also need to be negotiated and solved collectively. With a closer relationship between the party and government, this idea has gradually extended to the field of state governance.

For example, after the reform and opening up, China's decision-maker is no longer a single central government or a high-level government. The state has incorporated more and more grassroots elites and non-governmental organizations into the political system through systems such as political consultative conferences and democratic hearings. Government departments, social media, and think tanks can act as policy proposers and governance explorers, and then participate in the decision-making process on issues such as education, medical care, environmental protection, and public resource pricing. Thus, China's governance shows a wide range of consultation and democracy (Mertha, 2009).

Moreover, the central government strengthens the openness of political opportunity structure not only through specific democratic procedures. Its process of seeking governance wisdom from local governments also implies profound democratic values. From changes of power distribution in public administration, we can see that flexible and sufficient independent exploration of the local is based on the decentralization of governance authority. Different governance tools adopted by local governments, in turn, accumulate decision-making experience for the central. As for the central-local interaction in public governance, the local governments represent a policy network composed of multiple activists. The central government adopts multiple mechanisms to form collaborative management with the locals. This "extensive exploration and collective consultation" governance mechanism is an essential strategy informing the central-local chain of democratic value.

Then, we need to observe from a centralization perspective. We have found that the looseness of liberal democracy is an important reason for the failure of the third wave of democratization. From the constant transition of political power between autocracy and democracy in Egypt and Thailand, we can see that democracy free from constraints of procedures and institutions is easily twisted.

However, when we examined China's political landscape, we found that the democratic connection between the government and society or the central and local governments did not lead to the country's division. China's democracy can be well governed, and the governance mechanism that plays a crucial role is the guidance given by the central. Under the principle of democratic centralism, the focus of centralization and democracy complement each other. It requires subordinate organizations to obey the superiors and the minority's preference to collective interests. In reality, the central inspects and decides the decentralized practice of democratic exploration throughout the country. Then, it promotes local governance tools and experience that has succeeded with outstanding achievements and sustainable development nationwide utilizing superiors' guidance and top-level promotion to ensure the adaptability and viability of state governance in the process of national transformation.

Nowadays, China's governance system and capacity are transforming to suit modernization. The top-down administrative system reform and the emerging local self-governance innovations are both exploratory trials on governance transformation. However, not all governance tools in use have positive feedback and value for promotion. Some scholars have begun to evaluate and reflect on the governance innovation activities of local governments, believing that substantive false innovations are inefficient, valueless, short-sighted, and highly repetitive. All these characteristics will lead to the waste and abuse of local governance resources.

Thus, the central government has been distinguishing the experience of local governments in the case they develop "substantive innovation" into "false innovation." Thereby, the central government can make choices in adopting guiding principles of national governance transformation. For example, in recent years, the grid-based governance model of some local governments and the information governance technologies of some municipal governments, after receiving the attention and recognition of the central government, have become models in other regions. A series of single or national cases highlight the role of the central government in advancing the modernization of the governance system.

It can be concluded that the combination of democracy and centralization corresponds to the transformation between centralization and decentralization, the latter tends to rectify the governance, while the former tends to build a more coordinated central-local relationship. Then, why can democracy and centralism coexist in harmony in China? We believe that the inclusiveness of the system plays a key role. First, the coexistence of formal and informal systems provides space for the integration of democracy and centralism.

Although the central government authorizes local governments to govern, there are no clear boundaries for any "authority". Thus, local governments will adopt many informal systems under the central's formal system to achieve effective governance. For example, the local governments increase the types of taxation and seek political support through everyday communications between upper and lower levels. The coexistence of formal and informal systems highlights the inclusiveness of China's governance. Because such informal systems are permitted by the central, local governments can consult and negotiate with the central by practical governance actions.

Second, the inclusiveness of the system is also reflected in the enhancement of the non-government subjects' ability to participate in governance. With further development in governance theory, multiple issues, network nodes, and decentralized cooperation have become the theoretical paradigms that scholars in political science and management science are keen to advocate. Each academic system emphasizes the role of social forces in governance. In China, public-participation-oriented governance reform shows a bottom-up dimension (Zang & Zhang, 2019). The closer to the grassroots government, the better the public participation in governance. And this inclusive governance also indirectly promotes local governments' autonomy and constantly improves its dominant position in national governance.

To sum up, the combination of local democratic exploration and centralized guidance is the essence of China's governance mechanism. Both are essentially institutional governance that maintains the authority of the state and government. Its governance discourse system is highly malleable. Although state governance, government governance, and social governance are different, the inclusiveness of China's political system can integrate them in a way of coordinating democracy and centralization, which also highlights the experience of China's governance mechanism.

5 Future Challenges and Trend of China's Governance

Francis Fukuyama once regarded Western democracy as the end of the history of political system development. Nevertheless, the fragility of emerging democracies and the rise of China's international status prove that his views overemphasize the procedural value of politics and ignore the reality of governance, which may lead to misjudgments by leaders. The governance mechanisms and context of different countries are constantly developing and evolving. Developed democracies began to pursue equal status among other social classes after completing their primitive accumulation of capital. While non-democratic countries prefer the authority of government and the ruling party, people's livelihood and government effectiveness are also the foundation for stable governance.

Therefore, different countries and polities have their appropriate governance model. At this stage, we cannot assert which kind of governance paradigm is necessarily correct. Despite today's relatively peaceful international context, China's governance and development face multiple challenges. It is necessary to have a clearer understanding of the development trend of China's governance and positively distinguish and deal with various potential challenges.

First, there are still uncoordinated and unbalanced factors in China's central-local relationship. Shaun G. Breslin once pointed out that China's political and economic decentralized governance cannot fully implement the national development policy. There are differences in terms of development and policy environment among China's regions. And local governments often distort or even resist the central's policy (Breslin, 1996). Even now, the distortion of the central policies is still common. For example, financial conflicts between the central and the local in China's real estate industry have led to the local governments' dependence on land resources development. The central government's weakening control over the real estate industry has also aggravated the imbalance of the central-local relationship (Li et al., 2011). At the same time, although China's central government often uses decentralization and economic assistance to narrow regional development gaps, it may weaken the development of less-developed regions because the central government lacks effective performance assessment methods for ethnic minority areas (Wong & Takeuchi, 2013).

Second, there are still deficiencies in the systems of China's economic development. Chalmers Johnson once conducted an in-depth study of Japan's Ministry of Trade and Industry and then proposed that the main feature of a developmental state is that it rationally intervenes in economic development with a small-scale, meritocratic government. Subsequently, the developmental state theory is often used to study the Chinese government's intervention in the market. But China's state-owned economic sectors failed to provide sufficient financial guarantees to non-state-owned enterprises, which provided room for improvement in the vitality of non-state-owned enterprises (Leftwich, 1995). The politics-business relationship in China relies on interpersonal relationships and informal communication, lacking the guarantee of formal systems (K. S. Tsai, 2004). Moreover, due to the poor development of Chinese social organizations, the government's large-scale economic and social governance behaviors have indirectly led to a generally low social trust (Howell, 2006).

Third, China's technological governance was also questioned by international academics. From the perspective of technical determinism, scholars believe that the Internet and mobile information technology are powerfully reshaping China's politics, economy, society, and culture. In particular, Internet 2.0 has increased the openness of China's political opportunity structure, which reduced the organizational costs of social members and improved the vitality of social networks (Goodman et al., 1998). However, political competition, social integration, and value reconstruction will challenge China's political order (Zheng & Wu, 2005). Although some researchers believe that Internet technology can neither trigger China's political reforms nor improve China's system design level, technological governance with social penetration and political control may cause an increase of contentious incidents (Herold, 2009).

In addition, other foreign researchers have challenged China's governance from perspectives of decreased ideological intervention, the negative externality of economic growth, and the corruption of administrative departments (W.-H. Tsai, 2016). These are all fields in which China needs to improve in the future.

After reflecting on China's governance mechanism, we can find that governance subjects' perspective. However, China's governance is currently under the party's leadership and the government; many researchers are still trying to find ways for non-government entities to participate in governance. Especially, rural areas and communities are the focus of research (Holbig & Gilley, 2010). As for the driving force of governance reform, development with innovation is a crucial strategy for China to move toward governance modernization.

How to improve the sustainability of governance innovation is a common dilemma for local governments. In addition, since the central government strengthened the constraints on local governments' self-governance after the 18th National Congress of the CPC, the intensity of governance innovation has been reduced, which has become another bottleneck in the reform of China's governance system. In terms of governance tools, campaign-oriented governance is an effective means for China to solve unexpected problems.

However, since it is essentially the centralization and redistribution of local governance authority, it is destructive to the operation of the local bureaucratic system. Therefore, how to improve local governance efficiency on the premise of ensuring the central government's authority is a significant challenge for China's governance development. Concerning governance effects, poverty alleviation is the focus of top-level design in recent years, and targeted poverty alleviation policy is also being thoroughly carried out. However, from the perspective of its effects, technology-oriented governance and its increasing contents and requirements are detrimental to the actual work of poverty alleviation, which has caused a severe mismatch between macroscopic objectives and microcosmic performance in China's governance.

Albert O. Hirschman has suggested that the loyalty and advocacy of an organization is an essential factor in stimulating the vitality and sustainability of the organization (Hirschman, 2002). For a country, local advocacy is also a vital factor in promoting a country's development. Therefore, the balance of power between the central and the local, the coordination of fiscal power, and administrative authority are vital for China's stability and development. However, there is still room for improvement in exploring a more rational central-local power boundary that aims to achieve a specific objective of macro-governance. Based on the diachronic changes of China's central-local relationship, this chapter has made a preliminary introduction to historical practice and a theoretical interpretation.

References

Bardhan, P. (2002). Decentralization of governance and development. *Journal of Economic Perspectives, 16*(4), 185–205.

Barnett, A. D. (1967). *Cadres bureaucracy and political power in Communist China.* New York: Columbia University Press.

Bingyang, L., & Qingwang, G. (2012). Why China's tax revenue is likely to maintain its rapid growth: An explanation within the framework of tax capacity and tax effort. *Social Sciences in China, 33*(1), 108–126.

Breslin, S. G. (1996). China: Developmental state or dysfunctional development? *Third World Quarterly, 17*(4), 689–706.

Cao, Z. (2011). The vertically decentralized authoritarianism and the mechanisms of political stability in China. *Sociological Studies, 1*, 1–40.

Feizhou, Z., & Xing, Y. (2009). From macromanagement to micromanagement—Reflections on thirty years of reform from the sociological perspective. *Social Sciences in China, 6*, 104–127.

Fukuyama, F. (1992). Asia's soft-authoritarian alternative. *New Perspectives Quarterly, 9*(2), 60–61.

Goodman, R., White, G., & Kwon, H.-J. (1998). *The East Asian welfare model: Welfare orientalism and the state*. London: Routledge.

Heilmann, S. (2008a). From local experiments to national policy: The origins of China's distinctive policy process. *The China Journal*, (59), 1–30.

Heilmann, S. (2008b). Policy experimentation in China's economic rise. *Studies in Comparative International Development, 43*(1), 1–26.

Heilmann, S., & Perry, E. J. (2011). *Mao's invisible hand: The political foundations of adaptive governance in China* (Vol. 17). Harvard University Asia Center, Cambridge, MA.

Herold, D. K. (2009). Cultural politics and political culture of Web 2.0 in Asia. *Knowledge, Technology & Policy, 22*(2), 89–94.

Hirschman, A. O. (2002). *Shifting involvements: Private interest and public action*. Mercer: Princeton University Press.

Holbig, H., & Gilley, B. (2010). Reclaiming legitimacy in China. *Politics & policy, 38*(3), 395–422.

Howell, J. (2006). Reflections on the Chinese state. *Development and Change, 37*(2), 273–297.

Huang, P. C. C. (2008). Centralized minimalism semiformal governance by quasi officials and dispute resolution in China. *Modern China, 34*(1), 9–35.

Landry, P. F. (2008). *Decentralized authoritarianism in China: The Communist Party's control of local elites in the post-Mao era*. Cambridge University Press, New York.

Leftwich, A. (1995). Bringing politics back in: Towards a model of the developmental state. *The Journal of Development Studies, 31*(3), 400–427.

Li, J., Chiang, Y.-H., & Choy, L. (2011). Central–local conflict and property cycle: A Chinese style. *Habitat International, 35*(1), 126–132.

Lieberthal, K., & Oksenberg, M. (1990). *Policy making in China: Leaders, structures, and processes*. Mercer: Princeton University Press.

Lu, N. (2018). *The dynamics of foreign-policy decisionmaking in China*. Oxfordshire: Routledge.

Lu, X. (2012). *Social structure of contemporary China*. Singapore: World Scientific.

Mertha, A. (2009). "Fragmented authoritarianism 2.0": Political pluralization in the Chinese policy process. *The China Quarterly, 200*, 995–1012.

Parsons, T. (2010). *Essays in sociological theory*. Simon and Schuster.

Shambaugh, D. (2001). The dynamics of elite politics during the Jiang era. *The China Journal*, (45), 101–111.

Tsai, K. S. (2004). Off balance: The unintended consequences of fiscal federalism in China. *Journal of Chinese Political Science, 9*(2), 1–26.

Tsai, W.-H. (2016). How 'Networked Authoritarianism'was operationalized in China: Methods and procedures of public opinion control. *Journal of Contemporary China, 25*(101), 731–744.

Walder, A. G. (1989). Social change in post-revolution China. *Annual Review of Sociology, 15*(1), 405–424.

Weingast, B. R. (1995). The economic role of political institutions: Market-preserving federalism and economic development. *Journal of Law Economics and Organization, 11*(1), 1–31.

Wong, S. H.-W., & Takeuchi, H. (2013). Economic assistance, central–local relations, and ethnic regions in China's Authoritarian Regime. *Japanese Journal of Political Science, 14*(1), 97–125.

Xu, C. (2011). The fundamental institutions of China's reforms and development. *Journal of Economic Literature, 49*(4), 1076–1151.

Xufeng, Z., & Hui, Z. (2018). Social policy diffusion from the perspective of intergovernmental relations: An empirical study of the urban subsistence allowance system in China (1993–1999). *Social Sciences in China, 39*(1), 78–97.

Zang, L., & Zhang. (2019). *Re-understanding of contemporary Chinese political development*. New York: Springer.

Zheng, Y., & Wu, G. (2005). Information technology, public space, and collective action in China. *Comparative Political Studies, 38*(5), 507–536.

Zhou, L.-A. (2016). The administrative subcontract: Significance, relevance, and implications for intergovernmental relations in China. *Chinese Journal of Sociology, 2*(1), 34–74.

Zhou, X., Lieberthal, K., & Lampton, D. M. (1993). Bureaucracy, politics, and decision making in post-Mao China. *Contemporary Sociology, 22*(2), 186.

2 How Can China Implement Its Policies through Special-Issue-Oriented Governance (SIOG)

The Potential Governance Type

1 Research Background

"Governance" is a ubiquitous but complicated concept. As a concept frequently used in social media, the number of peer-reviewed publications on governance-related topics has also grown exponentially since the 1980s, according to the statistics of Google Scholar and China National Knowledge Infrastructure (CNKI). A growing proportion of governance papers are being released both at home and abroad. For instance, there are 4.6 million search results (in Chinese) on the keyword "governance" in CNKI, compared with 2.6 million English results in Google Scholar.[1]

Most researchers acknowledge that the improvement of governance capacity would contribute to the economic growth of developing countries. Chinese Scholars published many pieces on governance; however, they have not brought the public a better understanding of China's political development reality. On the one hand, existing Western theories could not fully explain China's reality. The blind quotes of foreign governance or political views reflect the political relevance gap, which has become a ubiquitous phenomenon recently (Wood, 2014). For example, the political theories could not adequately explain changes such as the fall of communism in 1989, the color revolution in the Arab world in 2011, and Chinese reform and opening up (Cheng & Fewsmith, 2008; Howard & Walters, 2014).

On the other hand, exogenous theories could not explain China's practice, and researchers have not created new effective endogenous theoretical paradigms from China's political and social development. So, there is always the theory deficit in the China's political development. Perhaps, it is the complexity of China's political development that has led to such a situation, which has undermined the significant intellectual contribution of Chinese scholars to the world, and reduced

DOI: 10.4324/9781003363712-2

the value of Chinese political science research. From the microcosmic viewpoint, the policy and institution of China in practice haven't been fully carefully studied based on universal academic criteria and standards. From the macroscopic viewpoint, we cannot objectively compare and draw on lessons from the complex progress of different countries based on China's reality. The practical experience and theoretical conclusions of China's development cannot be considered the extant academic contends of political science.

Governance is mentioned in political science and so many fields, making its definition inaccessible and increasingly unclear. Just like Jessop said, it has enjoyed a remarkable revival over the last 15 years or so in many contexts; however, becoming a ubiquitous "buzzword" can mean anything or nothing (Jessop, 1998). In this case, an appropriate research strategy is to classify governance according to the practice of different countries, because governance is undoubtedly an overly rigid concept that cannot explain the performance of a country (Persson & Tabellini, 2006). Countries like China achieved eye-catching development without regime change or "good governance" with Western standards (Bell, 2016). A good level of governance with effective public administration could be more important for state development. Few pieces of research examined how states use power and implement policies in China recently.

Therefore, we pursue a theoretical paradigm to unscramble the various developments of other countries and focus on the theoretical explorations of governance indigenization. This chapter argues that SIOG is a common and unique political tool in China's political system, but it has been ignored by academics, and it fails to provide a new perspective for better understanding China's political progress and for promoting the theoretical dialogue between China's political practice and other countries' development. The second part analyzes the different governance types and their influences on China's studies. The third part points out difficulties in applying various governance types and practices of SIOG in modern China. The fourth part introduces the implementation and (dis)advantages of SIOG. The final piece is the conclusion of the whole chapter.

2 Governance and Its Types in Chinese Academic Community

2.1 Good Governance and Its Critics in China

This part mainly introduces and compares the research status quo of different governance types in China. In the governance family tree, good governance is the most discussed one. Learning from the practical experience of development-driven countries at the end of the 20th century, international scholars paid more attention to good governance. Meanwhile, because of the Asian economic crisis in 1997, global discussions about Asian values declined, intensifying the diffusion of good governance in politics. In fact, since the 1980s, aid donors or international organizations have often imposed reforming pressures on aid recipients to interfere with their policy-making through listing good governance performances as subsidiary conditions (Deborah et al., 2007; Lebovic & Voeten, 2009), especially stating good governance improvements and reforms essential for the public utility loan.

Like the World Bank, some international organizations regarded good governance as a universal type in government reform (Williams & Young, 2010; Woods, 2000). It mainly emphasizes certain features in developing countries, such as transparent policy-making and political participation system, clean and open government, professionalism in a bureaucratic system, responsible departments, steady and well-organized participation of civil society, full-fledged legal system, effective administrative system, and political mobilization in the mass campaign. Such good governance has also become a prerequisite for aids from international organizations and developed countries, making it crucial in international aid negotiations.

However, while governance is regarded as a positivistic concept to analyze the question "what it is," good governance is a standard for one to explore "what it should be." Although some international organizations have mentioned the abstract features of good governance, governance still cannot ignore the cultural and historical backgrounds of different countries. Since good governance is not just a simple operational blueprint, it should come from negotiations or agreements between stakeholders in different geographic contexts and policy networks.

With international organizations worshiping and practicing good governance worldwide, scholars shouldn't just blindly echo or support theory. Some good governance theories were criticized for their vague statements, lack of logic, or inappropriate hypotheses. Related views were empty talks, simplistic common senses, or unpractical illusions (Godbole, 2004). What's worse, institutions that enthusiastically promoted good governance even cannot meet the requirements themselves. Consequently, good governance was applied by most aid donors or international organizations in groundless, arbitrary, and one-sided ways.

These criticisms arising from unreasonable suitable governance applications were magnified in China and were regarded as a Western ideological and cultural invasion. Although many Chinese scholars advocated good governance, according to the search results in CSSCI (Chinese Social Sciences Citation Index) database, the number of papers on good governance was far smaller than papers about other governance types such as global governance.

In the past decade, global governance was always regarded as a practical entry-point in the comparative studies of international politics and an effective theory to promote agreements in international affairs (Hall & Biersteker, 2002; Held & Mcgrew, 2002). Besides, it also conformed to the thoughts and preferences of Chinese leaders, especially when China continuously stressed its international image as a major responsible power. However, research on global governance emphasized the roles of non-government organizations (NGOs) and that civil society should play crucial roles in global governance to weaken the government's power, which was the opposite of China's official ideology. For instance, the Chinese government has realized the actual threats caused by a rising civil society. As a result, the concepts of civil society and universal values were forbidden to be discussed in publications or researches, as regulated in an official document by CPC in 2013.[2]

2.2 Multi-level Governance and Interactive Governance

The researches on good governance and global governance faced dilemmas in China. The rapid progress of regional integration globally helped multi-level governance, emerged in Europe, to spread worldwide. Multi-level governance was once used as a theoretical perspective to explain or describe EU cohesion (Hooghe & Marks, 2003; Pentland, 1997). Then scholars found that under the EU Cohesion Policy, the interactions among multiple levels of management drove the political and economic developments of the EU.

With a land area similar to that of Europe, China is also faced with unbalanced development in different fields. Chinese scholars were quickly drawn to the EU's experience of multi-level governance, which attempted to grapple with the dilemma of the EU's grey area between intergovernmental and ultra-nationalism. However, multi-level governance was only the EU's practical experience, which was unsuitable for China's reality. For example, in China, local governments often lack sufficient budget or authority to make policies.

Especially in the information age, governments cannot fully implement policies without external support, reflecting a high degree of interdependence among governments, enterprises, NGOs, and civil societies. As cooperation among different governance subjects became increasingly important, a new governance type, interactive governance, was created.

Interactive governance, proposed by Professor Jurian Edelenbos (2010), meant that stakeholders (including relevant people and organizations) participate in different phases of policy-making to be more effective in planning and operational processes of more complicated projects and turn policy-making into a more integrated and participatory one. Therefore, this governance was also defined by Kooiman as a specific behavior in which people took measures to solve the governance obstacles to find a new strategy for a better governance goal (Kooiman et al., 2005). In the earlier age, it was named participatory governance, which indicated changed relations among public, private, and voluntary organizations in different areas, stressing the participation of multiple public departments. But this type governance, which would improve the quality and outcome of projects and political proposals through the interaction among participatory stakeholders, was different from central authorities established in traditional and hierarchical countries. Besides, it also required that government officials conform to it instead of holding back public opinion. Under the guidance of political participants, ordinary citizens would be turned into more active voters or supervisors to reduce their resistance in the actual implementation stages.

Interactive governance includes three ideal types: top-down governance, self-governance, and co-governance. Nevertheless, people lack sufficient experience or knowledge to become empowering political participants, so this type of governance was not feasible in China. NGOs cannot exercise their potential.

2.3 Adaptive Governance

Adaptive governance, a concept derived from environmental governance, which emphasizes resource management cooperation in response to the complexity and uncertainty of environmental changes (Chaffin et al., 2014). Scholars adopted the concept to interpret China's political economy. K. S. Tsai (2006) proposed that the adaptive informal institutions served as a vital intermediary in explaining China's institutional change. Perry and Heilmann pointed out that a succession of post-Mao leaders adopted an adaptive pattern of authoritarian rule and guerrilla policy-making style to withstand challenges (Perry & Heilmann, 2011). Adaptive governance emphasizes governments' policy experimentation and adaptability to reduce uncertainties and risks. The experimentation-based policy-making process stimulated policy learning and adjustment. Central leaders adopted a learning system to implement the CPC's necessary regime adjustments (W. H. Tsai & Dean, 2013).

Adaptive governance concentrates on the policy-making stage to interpret policy and institutional changes. The government adopts policies based on experimentation and learns to reduce policy risks. The central government promotes policy initiatives nationwide based on feedback from local governments. However, the theoretical framework of adaptive governance may be limited to only interpreting the policy implementation and possible policy outcomes.

We have been scrutinizing different types of governance. A great variety of views have been documented over the past several decades, ranging from conventionally westernized evolutionism to transformative ideas regarding institutional incongruity, technologist, or mixed historical institutionalism. They have adopted three essentially distinctive modes of argumentation. Some Chinese researchers place an overwhelming emphasis on unique Chinese characteristics, working in tandem with the publicity of the Communist Party, which strives to build confidence in China's socialist path and the commitment to the great "Chinese Dream." In contrast, others don't agree on the alleged uniqueness of Chinese characteristics and suggest that modern technologies in governance have a universal impact leading to convergence among different countries where there will inevitably be a diversity of regulations on information flows.

At the same time, some scholars have proposed a compromise between the above two viewpoints. On the one hand, they argue that China's governance nowadays is profoundly conditioned by historical contexts and that it might take several decades to achieve proper institutional arrangements. On the other hand, China is reluctant to fall behind its competitors in terms of economic development. Hence, the project of economic reforms, driven by the external demand of economic globalization, has been proceeding more quickly than the pace of political reforms.

No matter how much we refer to China's unique or universal characteristics, it is still necessary to figure out whether Chinese governance has been, to some extent, affected by pressures from international developments or the country's own historical, cultural, and ideological contexts. The features of Chinese political practice need to be further researched so that the next part will analyze an ordinary tool in Chinese practice—SIOG.

3 The Practice of Governance in China: The Case of SIOG

SIOG in China means that the government, in accordance with relevant laws and regulations, coordinates public officials in different departments to solve major social and economic problems within a limited time. Such as reducing the local crime rate, promoting stable social and economic development, ensuring social security, and maintaining the effectiveness of governance. Taking an example, for some time, several briberies and official misconducts were found in China's infrastructure and public service sectors, arousing severe public criticism. Under such situations, CPC would always choose SIOG to quell public opinions temporally.

Reports of China's supreme organ of power, the NPC, first mentioned SIOG in 1987. After that, this concept was constantly cited, and its application correspondently extended. In the beginning, the government mainly used it to prevent officials from corruption. Then, this tool was gradually expanded into other fields, for example, to improve farmers' income or deal with environmental pollution (Table 2.1).

As a specific tool for government policy implementations and the CPC's departments, SIOG is also widely adopted by different levels of government. The search of SIOG on official websites of municipal-level governments yields 56,831 items in relevant notices and announcements, 3,384 on the central government websites, and 73 from the State Council Gazette.[3] It shows that, on average, the central government carries out seven SIOG operations every year (Figure 2.1). The government mainly uses SIOG to control and discipline the behavior of bureaucrats. Besides, it extends SIOG to a broader range of issues like environmental governance. We calculated the media exposures of SIOG since 2007 and found a sharp increase in the number of SIOGs on social and economic developments, compared with that in political fields.

The numerous applications of SIOG have drawn great attention from scholars. SIOG can be considered a policy tool for governments to achieve specific goals in a particular time period. In existing studies about SIOG, most scholars regarded it as an informal government system adopted by CPC and the government or a way to mobilize people. For example, the Chinese government continuously put great efforts into applying SIOG to anti-corruption and the management of government vehicles. Unexpectedly, the news media reports and accurate responses from the public showed that the practical results had not met the expectations. That was why many scholars took SIOG just as a rush and campaign-oriented governance rather than an effective and

Table 2.1 The frequency of SIOG in CPC documents

Time	*Frequency*	*Topics of SIOG and the number of every topic*
The 13th National Congress of the CPC (1987)	1	Rectifying malpractice in governmental behaviors (1)
The 14th National Congress of the CPC (1992)	3	Preventing the violations of legal benefits of the public (2), Administrative charge (1)
The 15th National Congress of the CPC (1997)	5	Reducing the burden of farmers (4), Malpractice of officials (1)
The 16th National Congress of the CPC (2002)	14	CPC, administrative and industry behavioral regulations (5), Construction of a clean government (3), Internet governance (2), Environmental protection (2), Social, legal system and public security (1), avoiding the impediments of interests of the masses and reducing the burden of farmers (1)
The 17th National Congress of the CPC (2007)	9	Protecting the legal benefits of the public (3), Construction of a clean government (3), Internet governance (1), Commercial bribe (1), Construction of CPC, administrative and industry behavioral regulations (1)
The 18th National Congress of the CPC (2012)	5	Food safety (1), the mass line (consulting the masses) and mass perspective (1), The Eight-point Regulation for anti-corruption (Chinese: Baxiang Guiding 八项规定) (1), Party personnel assignments and political party building (1), Environmental protection and air pollution (1)

Note: The authors form the chart above: Selected vital documents of the 13th National Congress of the CPC, People's Publishing House, 1993; Selected key documents of the 14th National Congress of the CPC, People's Publishing House, 1996; Selected key documents of the 15th National Congress of the CPC, People's Publishing House, 2001; Selected key documents of the 16th National Congress of the CPC, People's Publishing House, 2005; Selected key documents of the 17th National Congress of the CPC, Central Party Literature Press, 2009; Selected key documents of the 18th National Congress of the CPC, People's Publishing House, 2017.

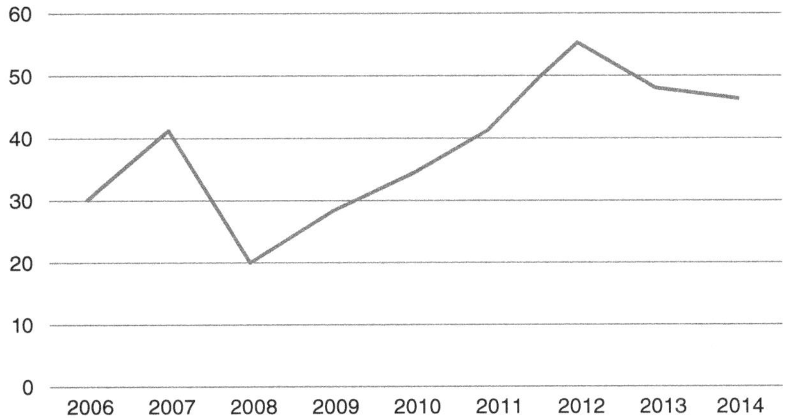

Figure 2.1 The frequency of SIOG in the State Council Bulletin

Note: The total number of the term "SIOG" in "regulations, opinions, notices and decisions" issued by the State Council.

steady legal system. This chapter will further analyze the implementation process and (dis)advantages of SIOG in the following parts.

4 The Implementation Process of SIOG

The implementation of SIOG encourages phased nationwide rectifications of specific issues through a powerful administrative system that uses particular offices, documents, financial resources, and the training of designated personnel to coordinate among different departments and different levels of governments. In practice, SIOG can be divided into three levels according to its target at national, regional, or local issues. National SIOG often has greater influences and more typical characteristics, as the central government can mobilize more financial resources, media resources, and human resources. In this part, we discuss SIOG mainly at the national level.

The frequent use of SIOG as a policy tool produces a large number of cases. For example, during the 2008 global financial crisis, China launched the Economic Stimulus Program, one of China's most significant economic events over the past decade. The Chinese government put forth an economic stimulus package of 4 trillion RMB ($586 billion) to minimize the global financial crisis's impact on China and stimulate economic growth (Ouyang & Peng,

2015). After the Sichuan earthquake in 2008, ten SIOG methods were implemented to boost domestic consumption and promote economic development, aiding infrastructure constructions and post-earthquake reconstructions.

In addition, as corruption in the construction sector is rampant in China (Yongnian & Gang, 2016), a large number of public investments ended up with business fraud and local governments' malpractice. The central government noticed these problems, and in July 2009,[4] it decided to launch a SIOG to address these issues in the construction industry for two years. It targeted six areas with highlighted risks and issues: decision-making inspection, tendering and bidding investigation, approval, and transfer of mining rights of the land, planning management and environmental influence evaluation, capital management, and quality management of construction projects. A central leading group was established to govern prominent problems in engineering constructions, with the leader being the vice general secretary of the Central Commission for Discipline Inspection (CCDI). The major members consisted of 19 ministers or commissioners. In addition, video and telephone conferences were employed to mobilize local governments to ensure policy implementations. Particular websites, offices, and hotlines were established to supervise the behavior of officials and respond to potential problems.

What's more, the leading group issued official documents to instruct and regulate policy implementations systematically. After a while, the upper-level government launched a full-scale inspection to evaluate the policy's effectiveness and rectify improprieties. An annual summary and outlook were used to predict problems and explore future mechanisms.

Since the launch of SIOG in engineering constructions, the central government has introduced 97 documents of regulatory standards and 89 others to be listed in the project. Based on preliminary statistics from September 2009 to March 2011, the whole country has examined the use of state-owned capitals and 384,500 projects funded by government investments, with 244,400 wrongdoings spotted, of which 203,700 receiving ratifications. The national disciplinary inspection authorities have received 33,100 reports of discipline-and-law violations in the field of engineering constructions, of which 17,200 were registered, 15,600 closed, and 11,273 people received punishments from administrative and party discipline authorities, including 78 instances at the ministerial (bureau) level and 1,089 at the county (division) level. In addition, the national prosecuting authorities have registered and investigated 12,344 cases of crimes and 15,010 persons of interest in engineering constructions. There were 11,050 cases of corruption and bribery involving 13,416 people and 1,294 instances of wrongdoings and violations of rights concerning 1,594 people.[5] In the same period, similar project inspections made by auditing departments did not show much governance and effects.

The implementation mechanism of SIOG can be summarized from the cases mentioned earlier. The first step is to trigger SIOG, following a top-down policy process. Governmental attention is distributed to various policy topics. The outbreak of social and economic problems draws the attention of the upper-level government, who then prioritize them for actions. These problems might be related to a wider range of issues, challenging social and political stabilities or economic developments. As a result, it is implausible for a single government sector to deal with them; typical standard administrative methods are inadequate under these circumstances. Therefore, it is essential to introduce the policy tool--SIOG.

The second step is to set up an organization. A SIOG leading group or special operations team is established to quickly coordinate multiple government sectors, make decisions and select possible policy options under the instructions of CPC and the Central Government.

After that, the team employs different tools for policy mobilizations and explains the importance of the policy is the form of video and telephone conferences. The leading group issues official documents to instruct policy implementations in the State Council or multiple ministries and commissions. Supervisory groups (mainly formed by CPC Commission for Discipline Inspection) are employed to inspect and monitor policy implementation.

In the end, the upper-level government evaluates the effectiveness of the policy and holds a summary and a commendation conference. In this process, the government summarizes effective detailed mechanisms to improve the effectiveness of subsequent policies. The typical cycle of SIOG is depicted in Figure 2.2.

Indeed, each static analysis can only provide a highly simplified explanation of complex social phenomena. It cannot be guaranteed that the mechanism will match all SIOG practices, such as regional and local practices mentioned before.

Undoubtedly, integrating departments in SIOG and inter-government cooperation in Western countries are not the same thing. In particular, the developing countries don't have a mature bureaucracy system, so SIOG is a step to mature bureaucratic systems. It improves the efficiency of department segmentations as much as possible. China, as the biggest developing country, is still transforming from

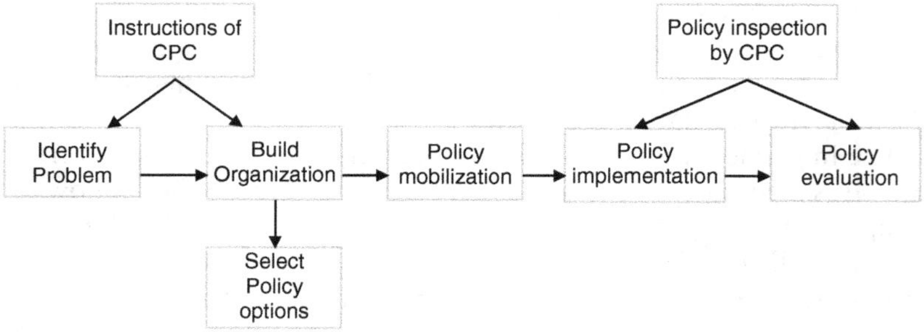

Figure 2.2 The cycle of SIOG

a traditional agricultural society to a modern industrial one. During this process, imbalanced development between urban and rural areas, among different regions as well as social classes stood out. Obstacles such as the lower level of various per capita indexes, improper economic structures, and flaws in the existing systems and mechanisms are gradually hampering further developments.

Therefore, economic development remains a long-term task. The constant reduction of administrative expenses will become an irreversible trend, and maximizing the governance effect with limited administrative costs will become an urgent issue for authorities from top to bottom. Officials at all levels are familiar with the mode and mechanism of SIOG, which also lowers training and organizing expenses, thus achieving economic feasibility. The following part will discuss the advantages and disadvantages of SIOG.

5 Advantages and Disadvantages of SIOG

Maybe it is difficult for many people to understand why Chinese officials prefer this policy tool–SIOG. In the practice of China's government, the CPC needs to simultaneously and effectively address both the increasing needs of good governance and social demands; otherwise, its legitimacy will be undermined (Shambaugh & Brinley, 2008). China's governance structure has the characteristic of "fragmented authoritarianism": the institutional cleavages and fragmentations of both authorities and resources make policy implementation vulnerable to vertical and horizontal agencies (Mertha, 2009). The Chinese model of local governance under reform has been remarkably flexible at the sheer level, but the evolution of inter-government relations demonstrates a surprising degree of institutional autonomy.

Of course, the discretionary power is of great importance for the government, however, it also accounts for the abuse of power as well as (Paler, 2005). It is costly and infeasible for the upper-level government to monitor the behavior of local officials and enforce policy implementations, especially in the context of selective policy implementations and collusion among local governments (O'Brien & Li, 1999). To achieve effective local governance, the central government needs a wider range of channels and networks to evaluate local performances and facilitate institutions of central-local communications. At the horizontal level, complementary tasks are grouped separately for specialized horizontal institutions, and massive overlaps of bureaucratic authorities and overly specific rules leading to low efficiencies. Therefore, the central government needs to coordinate across ministries.

For China, SIOG integrates with policy-makings and implementations and attempts to overcome the bureaucratically complex problem of fragmentation. It maximizes the advantages of matrix governance structures to achieve a specific policy goal. Such a structure consists of two intertwined and overlapping administrative systems, namely the vertical and horizontal systems. They both target fulfilling specific tasks (as shown in Figure 2.3). It is usually referred to as the *Tiaokuai* (integration of central government and those at different levels) system in Chinese. Under such a structure, SIOG can take advantage of strengths in all matrix units, coordinate their activities and match government functions with their capabilities. This structure is also relatively stable, so it can gather and distribute administrative resources effectively and satisfy the development needs in the rapid-transforming period of society.

Developing countries have technical and economic needs for SIOG and have a practical need entailed by their complex political and administrative environment. In most cases, developing countries usually face complex political situations. It is easier for policy-making organs to accept the SIOG strategy, making it possible to minimize impacts or interferences from relevant powers or interest groups. Thus, SIOG has become a convenient management method and policy tool for government departments to enforce and implement public policies. Reproduction and expansion of national power cast off the difficulty of choosing policy tools and help maintain the continuity and sustainability of legitimate political orders. The administrative context in China is quite complicated, with diversities, differences, and other factors responsible for various impacts on administrative activities at all governmental levels.

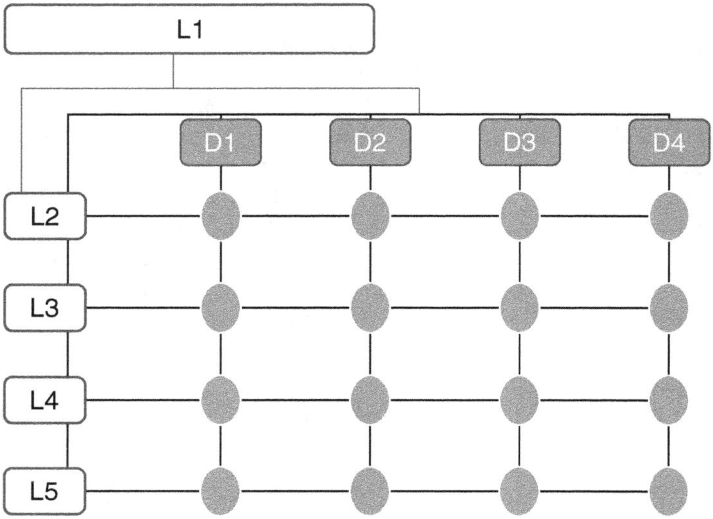

Figure 2.3 Model of the effects of matrix governance

Note: L2, L3, …, L5 refer to the vertical lines of authority over various sectors reaching down from central government ministries (Tiao). D1, D2, …, D4 refers to the horizontal level of authority of the government at the provincial or local level (Kuai).

Consequently, authorities have no better alternative but to choose SIOG, as this policy tool can survive and develop amid complicated administrative activities so that personnel recruiting can be achieved promptly. It aligns with the current administrative context and secures short-term cooperation among various departments.

Meanwhile, SIOG maximizes the self-satisfaction of the bureaucratic organization as a specific social and public organization. On the one hand, self-satisfaction refers to the spillover effect of enlarging government's interests during its implementation of policies and its management of service for the nation and society. On the other hand, its cognition toward policy tools and policy-making capabilities is based on comparing the real effects and the original expectations of governance management and services. With resource deficiency and insufficient system capability, the maximum governance effect helps meet the need of self-satisfaction and a sense of achievements of the cadre, which also demonstrates how the government is pursuing effectiveness and legitimacy. At the same time, SIOG suits the matrix as mentioned above governance structure.

However, there is no doubt that as a policy tool, China's SIOG is often criticized for disturbing legal systems, neglecting long-term government institutional construction, and it also brings about opinion divergence between officials' preference and the public's opposition (as shown in Table 2.2).

Despite good intentions, the leaders often neglect basic social facts when they implement their so-called "projects of improving human living conditions" and choose to carry on those projects regardless of possible negative impacts and undesired results. Simplistic implementations imposed by state power organs bring about environmental and social problems. Examined from no matter what perspective, every large-scale social process or event would be much more complicated than the blueprints we can make ahead of time (Scott, 1998).

This chapter argues that although SIOG has a glamorous "outfit" of distinct characteristics, meeting actual needs and having pronounced effects, it can still be optimized. It is possible to improve our policy implementation efficiencies as well as standards and reduce opposition to policy implementations. As János Kornai indicates, every system can rectify the huge and dangerous system characters inside it. Still, it can never totally overcome and eliminate such characters which are deeply rooted in the system and have an inclination to duplicate themselves (Kornai, 1992). The main disadvantages of SIOG are listed below.

First, SIOG overly focuses on specific issues even though it shares the basic characteristics of a matrix governance structure. Usually, practitioners' responsibilities are greater than their original power, and they may be subject to instructions from different superior organs. Since they are generally from various departments and their cooperation is temporary, the SIOG team leaders not have enough authority to make either encouragement or punishment based on their performances, decreasing the overall efficiency and stability of governance. Matrix governance measures that focus narrowly on policy power and efficiency often neglect negative effects on public rights caused by simplistic policy implementations. Even well-designed policies still contain some privileges or authorizations that exclude public opinion exchanges on key issues in the policy-making process. A hastily built SIOG structure can never fulfill the expectations that a policy should establish wide-range goals, stipulate mechanism arrangements, specify detailed and relevant powers, and regulate the rights of concerned personnel.

Second, SIOG overlooks the long-term institutional construction of government capabilities. Faced with governance inability, the

Table 2.2 The discrepancy between taxpayers and government officials

	Economy	*Efficiency*	*Accountability*	*Procedure legitimacy*	*Target*	*Flexibility*
Taxpayers	Expect to cut back the budget	Public service to satisfy individual needs	Be responsible for the public	Stick to procedure and targets	Clear; With reasonable intention; Directed by mandates	Keep closely on track with the social changes
Government officials	Expect to enlarge the budget	Public service to satisfy all social needs	Be responsible for the project or higher authorities	Result-oriented	Unclear	Can never freely explain institutional mandates, Instrumental enforcer

government can achieve short-term effects by implementing SIOG measures and indulging in self-satisfaction. It further uses such short-term effects as excuses to postpone political reforms and even ignore constructing a more reliable and standardized system. Gradually, instead of overall improvement of government capability, piecemeal fixes become the norm. To make matters worse, the government's dependence on such ways may be aggravated by the so-called "ratchet effect" (it's hard to turn around once a habit is formed), making it even harder to optimize the governance pattern. It is certain that, currently, the authorities have noticed such a disadvantage, and for nearly every SIOG, a long-term institution is called for. Researches on the phrase "long-term institution" (from 2000 until now) have found constant mentions in notices from the State Council, even more, frequent than the phrase "SIOG." However, in actual practice, establishing and implementing such a long-term mechanism still requires more effort.

Most SIOGs are ordered by the central government in the first place and then carried forward by governments at lower levels, which causes deficiencies of horizontal connections, imbalance of governance network structures, and inactive participation in grassroots governance, resulting in the bottleneck of policy implementations and the loss of capabilities and authorities for local governments. In addition, SIOG adopts a one-size-fits-all practice, allowing administrative controls to be above rules of law, and making it impossible to carry out and implement policies according to local conditions. Thus, the domination and legalization of undesirable hidden powers in government organs become unavoidable. Society is in a phase of transformation that emphasizes innovations in social management methods and requires diversified governance modes. Therefore, it is difficult for central-government-based SIOG to meet the demands of local management.

More significantly, dependence on SIOG can make it challenging to tackle social disputes from a long-term perspective and impede policy capabilities of sustainable developments and even fuel the speculation toward law-enforcement departments. All of these result in a lack of responsibilities, lazy administration, and even corruption in relevant departments that would rather spend the budget on temporary effects of SIOG to win people's praises.

This is also proof of the strange phenomenon described from another perspective by Simon Kuznets. He notes little government participation before a problem occurs and its laissez-faire approach to any activities that violate the rules in the market, and, in contrast, much government interference in the market after a problem occurs, when the government would mobilize nearly all of its resources to tackle that problem and adjust all the market regulations to accommodate the solution. Both the government and the market have to pay a considerable price for solving that problem. Such a strange phenomenon can be seen in China's public policy practice, e.g., the successive ten-time SIOGs of "reducing the burden of farmers and protecting the interests of the masses" from the 14th to the 17th National Congress of the CPC, which achieved very few results even with such a high frequency of repetitions. And since 2000, as many as seven rounds of SIOG aimed at "reducing the burden of farmers" were cited in the State Council Gazette, and "Rectifying malpractice in various sectors" was even mentioned once every year.

SIOG also magnifies the part that the public plays in the administrative process. As it is inconsistent with the government's real intentions and requirements, it fails to meet citizens' expectations of more political participation, further undermining the coordination and communication between the government and the public. With strong irrationalities, people are easily affected by too many emotional factors and always hope that their goals can be achieved as expected. Usually, it boasts the public's participation. However, its effects decrease gradually with the increase in its usage and the loss of the masses' actual political efficacies, bringing down the overall impacts of governance. Therefore, prudence, speculation, and use of force in the process of SIOG make it an effective yet very delicate and troublesome policy tool.

6 Conclusion and Discussion

The traditional studies of sub-governance types mainly focus on their positive images and inner meanings, which stand specifically for the pursuit of an equal, fair, transparent, and reliable public life. In an institute lacking security and solidity and filled with corruption, poverty, and dysfunction of public service, good governance or multi-level governance constitutes practice guidance.

Its capabilities can never match its reputation, and various exceptions in this concept have made it redundant for promoting economic development, reducing poverty, improving community growth, and enhancing public participation and governmental responses. Therefore, scholars have pointed out that the concept of governance is increasingly swelling, resembling the shape of an umbrella (Piattoni, 2009). The idea of governance seems to have become an omnipotent protective cover as it reflects varied dimensions that are of interest to different supporters and provides supporting proofs for those concrete areas. To some extent, it has become the "fig leaf" for solving the development problems of all nations (Grindle, 2012).

In practice, reforms differ in countries. Western countries tend to believe that governance sometimes emphasizes the reform of public sectors and focuses on refining the resource distribution and coordination system. There is no such standard governance model that can adapt to every country and every field (Bevir et al., 2010). The creativity and uniqueness of governance practice in a specific country, such as SIOG, cannot be ignored. Simply put, through the various resources across multiple departments, SIOG is a supplemental toolkit for the defective Chinese policy implementation system during its difficult transition from central planning to a market economy and democratic rule. China has long historical traditions of bureaucratic rule and maintains a meritocratic system to recruit elites and sustain its rule (Fukuyama, 2013).

Since the establishment of the PRC in 1949, the Chinese government has demonstrated unprecedented capacity to formulate, implement, and monitor nationwide policy initiatives (Brandt et al., 2013). Strong state capacity endows government with unprecedented leverage for policy implementation. Historical traditions and socialism's legacy shape China's political institution. The governance practices in China can enrich our knowledge about governance patterns and operation mechanisms.

Compared with good governance, multi-level governance, cooperative governance, and so on (as shown in Table 2.3), SIOG emphasizes practical problem-solving. SIOG in public affairs focuses on the solutions to complex and thorny problems generated by the rigid bureaucratic system and social-economic developments. SIOG overcomes government fragmentations and the lack of capacities and accountabilities of the political leadership in developing countries.

The effective governance model should be based on diverse governance practices and specific rules that can be applied to all organizational circumstances. In practice, we cannot ignore the differences in both theory and practice between developing countries and developed countries. Otherwise, there will be a higher possibility of arbitrarily unobservable terms, ending with the complexity of a theory outstripping the real explanatory power. It might be easier for theorists to apply abstract or influential concepts to their specific researches to conclude how governance adapts to theories. Yet there is also a danger of having one-size-fits-all thinking or placing all on a procrustean bed.

Table 2.3 Characteristics of SIOG and comparison with other types

	Special-issue-oriented governance	*Good governance*	*Multi-level governance*	*Interactive governance*
Theoretical and practical background	The renewal of state autonomy and capacity building after the financial crisis in the 21st Century	The rise of NPM and civil society	European integration	Privatization of Public Sector; electronic government popularized
Advocate	Chinese scholars	International organizations	USA and EU scholars	EU scholars
Units of analysis/ space-time horizon	Area studies	Countries and area studies	Area studies	Area studies and communities
Theoretical presuppositions	pragmatism Rational politic man	Rational political man	Hierarchical orders	Hierarchical orders; rational economic man
Practices	China's reform and opening-up process, the practice of developmental states	WGI	EU	The innovation of cooperation government
Criteria for outcome	Deal with complex society effectively	Utilizing the resource, Promoting development	Equilibrium developmental goals	Consultation & consensus
The role of the state	Persist penetration	Withdrawn	Half withdrawn	Half withdrawn
Ideologies	Marxism	Weakening	Maintaining	Maintaining
Impact on the institutional level	Debureaucratization	Debureaucratization; decentralized	decentralized	Post-democratization; decentralized
Impact on the practical level	Government predominance	The rise of civil society; the government initiative	Ordered social participation; the government initiative	Individuals and organizations involved in dialogue and consultation; government coordination

Scholars have held different views based on different stands, pondering how to demonstrate China's developments and achievements and eliminate governance deficits as well (Pei, 2002; Vol., 2002). This chapter points out that SIOG is playing the role of a flexible facilitating agent rather than an overall commander in China. In addition, the practice of SIOG can be defined merely as a specific policy practice instead of a Chinese model. Besides, this policy practice can integrate national strengths with the processes of national constructions. For example, through analyses toward the Communist Party's Socialist Education Campaign (1962–1966), extant studies have offered a historical interpretation that the state-making process was a contest of bureaucratic and discursive practice between central and local regimes (Gries & Thornton, 2010).

Moreover, SIOG in economic development also emphasizes the combination of the government and the market. Taking SIOG in anti-poverty as an example, scholars have pointed out that thanks to a co-evolutionary process in which the market and government mutually adapt, China has achieved successes in economic development (Ang, 2016). Therefore, SIOG, as a potential analytical framework, can explain why bureaucrats in China are keen on using it when faced with weak institutions and imperfect development of China's market economy.

Frankly, it is not easy to make a dialectical judgment toward China's adaptation of governance based on a one-sided viewpoint or limited knowledge. Interdisciplinary works, varied approaches, and multiple operationalism are required to review and aim to understand China's future governance better. When we analyze the reality in China, what matters is not the approach we take, whether sticking to Chinese exceptionalism or insisting on the ideology of liberalism, but how we perceive the country.

In this chapter, the authors reveal impartial facts in comparative governance research and introduce a new governance type with Chinese characteristics. China provides a unique case for understanding a different kind of governance. This governance practice can enrich our knowledge about governance patterns and operation mechanisms. China has gone through a boom-bust cycle with the same cadre organization in different historical periods since 1949, irrespective of external factors. Consequently, it is difficult to put aside the temporal dimension when analyzing the performance of Chinese bureaucracy in a certain period. This chapter argues that SIOG has the advantage of absorbing a large number of talented elites. In contrast, a number of studies in China have shown that this prevailing practice in itself hinders innovative developments in other fields. Moreover, the flexibility of the cadre system and the expansion of discretion are the leading causes of corruption in today's China.

Notes

1 See details, https://scholar.google.com and http://www.cnki.net, access date: October 1, 2017.
2 Chris Buckley. China Warns Officials Against 'Dangerous' Western Values. *NY Times*. 2013-05-13. http://www.nytimes.com/2013/05/14/world/asia/chinese-leaders-warn-of-dangerous-western-values.html?ref=china.
3 The numbers above are summarized from 2000 to August 2011. The Gazette of the State Council of the People's Republic of China (hereinafter referred to as State Council Gazette) - edited and published by the General Office of the State Council - has been the official publication of the Chinese central government since 1955, with readers at home and abroad. The State Council Gazette consists of the following sections: Administrative regulations, resolutions and executive orders promulgated by the State Council; Decisions made by the State Council concerning organizational adjustments, changes of administrative areas, and official appointments and removals; Rules and regulations from government departments and agencies, as well as documents authorized for publication. According to the Law on Legislation of the People's Republic of China, the version appearing in the State Council Gazette shall be considered the official version.
4 The General Office of the CPC Central Committee and the General Office of the State Council issued the Opinions on Launching SIOG of Key Issues in Engineering Construction, http://fanfu.people.com.cn/GB/9893397.html.
5 http://news.cntv.cn/20110517/112407.shtml, access date: December 1, 2017.

References

Ang, Y. Y. (2016). *How China escaped the poverty trap.* Cornell University Press.

Bell, D. A. (2016). *The China Model: Political meritocracy and the limits of democracy.* Princeton University Press.

Bevir, M., Rhodes, R. A. W., & Weller, P. (2010). Comparative governance: Prospects and lessons. *Public Administration, 81*(1), 191–210.

Brandt, L., Ma, D., & Rawski, T. G. (2013). From divergence to convergence: Reevaluating the history behind China's economic boom. *Cage Online Working Paper, 52*(1), 45–123.

Bräutigam, D. A., & Knack, S. (2007). Foreign aid, institutions, and governance in Sub-Saharan Africa. *Economic Development & Cultural Change, 52*(2), 255–285.

Chaffin, B. C., Gosnell, H., & Cosens, B. A. (2014). A decade of adaptive governance scholarship: Synthesis and future directions. *Ecology & Society, 19*(3), 56.

Cheng, Y. N., & Fewsmith, J. (2008). *China's opening society: The non-state sector and governance.* Routledge.
Edelenbos, J. (2010). Institutional Implications of Interactive Governance: Insights from Dutch Practice. *Governance—An International Journal of Policy Administration and Institutions, 18*(1), 111–134.
Fukuyama, F. (2013). The origins of political order: From prehuman times to the French revolution. *Contemporary Sociology A Journal of Reviews, 42*(2), 207–209.
Godbole, M. (2004). Good governance: A distant dream. *Economic & Political Weekly, 39*(11), 1103–1107.
Gries, P. H., & Thornton, P. M. (2010). Disciplining the state: Virtue, violence, and state-making in modern China. *Perspectives on Politics, 8*(4), 1263.
Grindle, M. (2012). Good governance: The inflation of an idea. In B. Sanyal, L. J. Vale, & C. D. Rosan (Eds.), *Planning ideas that matter: Livability, territoriality, governance, and reflective practice* (pp. 259–282), Boston: MIT Press.
Hall, R. B., & Biersteker, T. J. (2002). *The emergence of private authority in global governance.* Cambridge: Cambridge University Press.
Held, D., & Mcgrew, A. G. (2002). *Governing globalization: Power, authority and global governance.* Cambridge: Polity Press.
Hooghe, L., & Marks, G. (2003). Unraveling the Central State, but how? Types of multi-level governance. *The American Political Science Review, 97*(2), 233–243.
Howard, M. M., & Walters, M. R. (2014). Explaining the unexpected: Political science and the surprises of 1989 and 2011. *Perspectives on Politics, 12*(2), 394–408.
Jessop, B. (1998). The rise of governance and the risks of failure: The case of economic development. *International social science journal, 50*(155), 29–45.
Kooiman, J., Bavinck, M., Jentoft, S., & Pullin, R. (2005). *Fish for life: Interactive governance for fisheries.* Amsterdam University Press.
Kornai, J. (1992). *The socialist system: The political economy of communism.* Princeton University Press.
Landry, P. F. (2008). *Decentralized authoritarianism in China.* New York: Cambridge University Press.
Lebovic, J. H., & Voeten, E. (2009). The cost of shame: International organizations and foreign aid in the punishing of human rights violators. *Journal of Peace Research, 46*(1), 79–97.
Mertha, A. (2009). "Fragmented Authoritarianism 2.0": Political pluralization in the Chinese policy process. *China Quarterly, 200*(200), 995–1012.
O'Brien, K. J., & Li, L. (1999). Selective policy implementation in rural China. *Comparative Politics, 31*(2), 167–186.
Ouyang, M., & Peng, Y. (2015). The treatment-effect estimation: A case study of the 2008 economic stimulus package of China. *Journal of Econometrics, 188*(2), 545–557.
Pei, M. (2002). China's governance crisis. *Foreign Affairs, 81*(5), 96–109.

Pentland, C. (1997). Cohesion policy and European integration: Building multi-level governance by Liesbet Hooghe. *International Journal, 52*(2), 382.

Perry, E. J., & Heilmann, S. (Eds.) (2011). Embracing uncertainty: Guerrilla policy style and adaptive governance in China. In *Mao's Invisible Hand: The political foundations of adaptive governance in China*. BRILL.

Persson, T., & Tabellini, G. (2006). Democracy and development: The devil in the details. *American Economic Review, 96*(2), 319–324.

Piattoni, S. (2009). Multi-level governance: A historical and conceptual analysis. *Journal of European Integration, 31*(2), 163–180.

Scott, J. C. (1998). *Seeing like a state: How certain schemes to improve the human condition have failed*. New Haven: Yale University Press.

Shambaugh, D. L., & Brinley, J. J. (2008). *China's communist party: atrophy and adaptation*. Berkeley: Univ of California Press.

Tsai, K. S. (2006). Adaptive informal institutions and endogenous institutional change in China. *World Politics, 59*(01), 116–141.

Tsai, W. H., & Dean, N. (2013). The CCP's learning system: Thought unification and regime adaptation. *China Journal, 69*(1), 87–107.

Vol., N. (2002). China's governance crisis. More than musical chairs. *Foreign Affairs, 81*, 96–109.

Williams, D., & Young, T. (2010). Governance, the World Bank and liberal theory. *Political Studies, 42*(1), 84–100.

Wood, M. (2014). Bridging the relevance gap in political science. *Politics, 34*(3), 275–286.

Woods, N. (2000). The challenge of good governance for the IMF and the World Bank themselves. *World Development, 28*(5), 823–841.

Yongnian, Z., & Gang, C. (2016). China's politics: Bold reforms and unabated war on corruption. *East Asian Policy, 08*(01), 16–24.

3 When China's Government Reforms Meet Western Administrative Theories

Do They Fit?

1 Introduction

Whenever scholars discuss the convergence and divergence of social science disciplines, it is often emphasized that the disciplines are related to cultural, institutional, historical, or social contexts. When we discuss the context of government reform, a key confusion arises about whether a one-size-fits-all theory derived from one country's development trajectory applies to different countries. Developing countries have carried out many reforms based on different academic theories to promote political and economic development, but they may not always achieve the desired results (Cheung, 1997; Meier et al., 2015).

In the field of public administration, developing countries still tend to adopt the current theories and principles from developed countries. Over the last 30 years, an increasing number of less-developed countries, as well as some developed counterparts (Dent, 2005), have implemented or reconstructed administrative reforms on the advice of their academic advisers, most of whom have been grounded on a liberalized weltanschauung. How to evaluate the effectiveness of reforms, in turn, has revitalized the classic debate among researchers (Andrews, 2013).

When we examine the Chinese bureaucracy, China employs the idea of a "democratic elite" and other Weber principles in its administrative practice to achieve governance goals (Rothstein, 2015). The impact of such reforms, in terms of their development path to improve governance, has been examined by a kaleidoscope of perspectives (Burns, 2000; Christensen et al., 2008; Haque & Turner, 2013; Ngok & Zhu, 2007; Su et al., 2013). However, since 1980s, waves of theoretical changes have occurred in the international public administration, notably, with the successive proposals of reinventing government theory, the entrepreneur government theory, the new public-service theory, the joint-up government theory, and so on. Accordingly, China

DOI: 10.4324/9781003363712-3

also saw six waves of institutional reforms in government from 1982 to 2015, and a government turnover followed each.

While much of the previous literature has documented these reform efforts through case studies and cross-sectional data analysis, few have attempted to assess the changes that have occurred over the past 33 years. Nevertheless, researchers either implicitly defended the effectiveness of western experience (theory) by arguing that the lack of relevant context factors and advanced market economy involvement in the top political echelons hinders the positive "imitation of the West" (Christensen et al., 2012), or chronologically diagnosed the cause for the formation of the complicated relationship between Western theories and China's actual trajectory, which is somewhat unlikely to breed independently indigenous doctrines (Zhang, 2017).

To highlight the strengths of our research while distinguishing it from other studies, we aim to address the following questions in this chapter: (1) What is the relation between China's public administration and the theory of western public administration? (2) Have China's administrative reforms, notably the administrative streamlining and the local policy, reached their intended targets? (3) What can other developing countries learn from China's administrative reforms?

The rest of the chapter is organized as follows: Section 2 reviews the development of foreign academic theories and China's administrative reforms. Section 3 introduces the changes in ministries and civil servants hired by the State Council. Section 4 points out lessons we can learn from China's governmental reforms. Section 5 concludes the chapter, providing some potential policy suggestions for other developing countries.

2 The Development of Western Public Administration Theories and Government Reforms in China

High government performance is considered a necessary condition for achieving and enhancing the political visibility of the ruling party and gaining civic support. Since World War II, most Western developed countries have undergone a significant process of administrative restructuring. The unexpectedly unfortunate response to the oil crisis of the 1970s, and many other public emergencies triggered by modern technology, exposed deep-seated flaws in the administrative structures of many countries. These lessons motivated them to cut public spending, streamline the public sector, and streamline public services to improve administrative efficiency and keep institutional strength alive. Theories on public administration had a profound impact on the worldwide movements of government institution restructuring. These renowned theoretical schools include the New Public Management thrived in the 1980s, Janet Denhardt and Robert Denhardt's New Public Service, and the ongoing public administration doctrine of David H. Rosenbloom and Elinor Ostrom.

In the 1980s, administrative reforms were carried out across the developed Western and newly industrialized countries, especially in the former Soviet Union and the Eastern European bloc, which were struggling to transition to a market economy. Since then, this global wave of administrative reorganization has been the focus of academic and public discussion.

Key concepts such as public accountability and organizational best practices were derived from the New Public Management (NPM) reforms of the 1980s, with the hope of bringing "a clear direction" to post-communist development. However, as political scientists have pointed out, these necessary conditions for reform (such as norms, economic power, positive partisan obligations, and size of government) have challenges in developing countries. Specifically, the researchers found that sustainable development efforts in late-developing countries are inevitably hampered by a series of difficulties, such as government fiscal crises, prolonged economic slowdowns, public sector inefficiencies, rising inflation, bureaucratic tyranny, cronyism relationships, lack of accountability, and corruption (Christensen & Lægreid, 2002; Minogue & Polidano, 1998).

Almost every country has an obsession: how should government reorganization adapt to the changing socio-political environment at home and abroad? The original intention of such reforms is to restructure government institutions to improve efficiency and the quality of public services. However, the experience of developed countries is often considered too general or even opaque to address the dilemma of inefficient governance in developing countries. As the NPM strategy spreads around the world, it is still accepted by many countries despite skepticism about its actual effect. This paradigmatic doctrine also played a role in China's 1994 tax-sharing system and public spending reforms (Osborne & Gaebler, 1992; Pollitt et al., 1998).

In recent decades, it is common for international organizations to adopt a universalist thinking mode and ignore regional specificities. This can be seen in proposals for the further deepening of reforms in China. The theme of the proposal in China remains the privatization of state-owned enterprises (SOEs), in line with the neoliberal creed that failed to function in the face of the US subprime mortgage crisis and the European debt crisis.

Scholars hold different views on developing countries' NPM reform practices. Their academic discussions can be divided into three stages, corresponding to different approaches. In the first stage, scholars focused on developing countries adopting NPM reforms from history and culture. In the second stage, with the acceleration of globalization and the rising academic trend of "bringing the institutions back in" (Weiss, 2003), they tended to adopt the perspectives of institutionalism and globalism/cosmopolitanism. They examined whether these countries should accept NPM reform practices. During the third phase, with the development of computer technology and other new technologies in the new century, contemporary trends like technological determinism and social constructivism became the focus of analysis on how the conventional centerpiece of NPM principles would work in tandem with the fast-changing situation in developing countries (Table 3.1).

In recent years, following a new round of institutional reforms in Western countries, developing countries have also actively promoted administrative restructuring with the hope of modernizing their institutional setting and increasing the efficiency of public services. China has benefited from Western academic theories in its reforms and has made efforts to improve institutional settings.

Table 3.1 Different perspectives in different periods

		Accept NPM reform in developing countries	*Prudently accept or hesitate to accept NPM reform in developing countries*
1st period	Historical Perspective	Hood (1991)	Waldo (1976)
	Culture Perspective	Hood and Peters (2004), Pillay (2008), Samaratunge et al. (2008)	Gendron et al. (2001)
2nd period	Institutional Perspective	Richard and George (2004)	Pollitt (2001)
	Globalization Movement	Kim et al. (2014)	Welch and Wong (1998)
3rd period	Technological Determinism	Askim et al. (2009)	Dunleavy et al. (2006)
	Social Constructivism	Kaboolian (1998)	Elias (2006)

Since the start of the reform and opening up in the late 1970s, China has conducted seven relatively large-scale administrative structural reforms. These reforms took place in 1982, 1988, 1993, 2003, 2008, and 2013, which is clear that every generation of the CPC leadership had its reform goal.

Combining domestic conditions and international experience, China's reform approach is similar to foreign, especially Anglo-Saxon reform (Caulfield, 2006; Foster, 2005). An academic survey argued that Chinese bureaucratic cultures and practices had transformed various Western approaches (Chan & Chow, 2007). To further discuss the relationship between Chinese reform and international theory, Table 3.2 shows that each stage of Chinese reform has strong links with international experience and academic theory.

Due to the knowledge demand for Western theories, macro-comparative research has emerged in Chinese academia. For example, many translations of renowned Western scholars' books since the CPC took power in 1949. These works contain James Buchanan's "government failure" Public Choice theory, Edward Quade's Policy Analysis theory, Osborne's theory of Enterprise Government, Denhardt's New Public Service theory, and Rosenbloom's multiple public administration theory, all of which have become very popular in the academic circles, and allowed Chinese researchers to refresh and redefine knowledge along with research norms. Several monographs and research series have also blossomed, elaborating on the middle-level or micro-level comparison between China and the others (Christensen et al., 2008). In addition, lessons from some unsatisfying reforms elsewhere have also been studied in China. These academic works have introduced and further contrasted the previous theories and practices in Western countries, thus providing examples and theoretical implications on the theme of commensurability to help stimulate debates against doctrinaire practices. As a result, academic research in this area fueled reflection on meta-theory, methodology, professionalism, and the importance of a global outlook.

However, many Sinologists have identified a somewhat perplexing paradox. On the one hand, in the words of official propaganda, China has long believed in its uniqueness and official self-confidence in determining its developmental trajectory and timetable. Given the expression of the country's five-year plans, the Party's propaganda system constantly emphasizes citizens' and scholars' confidence in socialist ideology. Some scholars also highlight the concept of "reform practices with Chinese characteristics" (Aufrecht & Bun, 1995; Huang, 2008; Warner, 2008), aiming to theoretically rationalize the old claim of the

Table 3.2 Major institutional reforms in China and international inspiration (theories and practices)

Party congress and plenary session of CPC	*Topics of institutional reform*	*International theories and practices (especially in Western countries) for guidance*	*Reform practice*
The 12th CPC Central Committee meeting (September 1–11, 1982) and its 7th Plenum (October 20, 1987)	Improve government efficiency Separate the role of the Party and the state, and make them operate independently	New Public Management Theory Reforms Practice by Margaret Thatcher and Ronald Reagan	On May 8, 1982, the 22nd session of the 5th Standing Committee of the National People's Congress (NPC) passed *the Resolution on Reform of Institutions under the State Council.*
The 13th CPC Central Committee meeting (October 25–November 1, 1987) and its 2nd Plenum (March 15–19, 1988)	Separate the role of the Party and the state Reform the cadre system Promote economic and political structural reforms Transform governmental function	Theory of Public Choice The practice of power decentralization in France, Japan, Germany, and the US in the 1980s	The 7th NPC passed *the Ordinance of Reform of Institutions under the State Council.*
The 14th CPC Central Committee (October 12–18, 1992) and its 2nd Plenum (March 5–7, 1993)	Accelerate the transformation of governmental functions Streamline administrative procedures and promote administrative efficiency E-government (i.e., the "Golden Project" of 1993)	Reinventing Government Theory Entrepreneur Government Theory Flattening management in the governmental organization The introduction of electronic government in the US in 1993	The 1st session of the 8th NPC approved *the State Council's Institutional Restructuring Plan.*

Party congress and plenary session of CPC	*Topics of institutional reform*	*International theories and practices (especially in Western countries) for guidance*	*Reform practice*
The 15th CPC Central Committee (September 12–18, 1997 and its 2nd Plenum (February 25–26, 1998)	State-owned enterprises (SOEs) reform Develop institutional features to accommodate the Socialist Market Economy with Chinese Characteristics Deliberate and adopt plans to restructure the State Council	Privatization and enterprise reform in the public sector worldwide	The 1st session of the 9th NPC approved *the State Council's Institutional Restructuring Plan.*
The 16th CPC Central Committee (November 8–14, 2002) and its 2nd Plenum	Deepen reforms of governmental institutions to function in a more well-coordinated, equitable, transparent, and efficient pattern Deliberate and adopt Opinions on Deepening the Reform of Administrative System and Institution	The New Public Service Theory Development of Western civil society (e.g., community residents' participation in public affairs and policy-making) and advocacy of transition to polycentric governance	The 1st session of the 10th NPC adopted *the State Council's Institutional Restructuring plan.*
The 17th CPC Central Committee (October 15–27, 2007) and its 2nd Plenum (February 25–27, 2008)	Accelerate the reform of the administrative system to build a service-oriented government Adopt the Opinions on Deepening the Reform of the Administrative System and Plan for Restructuring	Theories of Whole-of-government, joined-up government, horizontal government, collaboration government	The 1st session of the 11th NPC adopted *the State Council's Institutional Restructuring Plan.*
The 18th CPC Central Committee (November 08–14, 2012) and its 2nd Plenum (February 26–28, 2013)	Super ministry system reform Government organizations integration	Theories of whole-of-government, joined-up government	The 1st session of the 12th NPC adopted *the State Council's Institutional Restructuring Plan.*

superiority of the socialist system and to internalize the perception that China's featured reforms did produce specific policy outcomes.

On the other hand, Chinese officials and think tanks have never stopped resorting to international theories and practices for designing and implementing domestic institutional reforms. For example, a growing consensus is that China is a theory consumer, not a proposer or provider. This situation implies that the localization of academic research, both an intellectual and a politics-driven catchphrase long advocated in China, has mostly failed.

How did China's administration reform practices absorb western theories? It drew on the administrative experience of their developed counterparts regardless of potential cultural incompatibilities (Bhagat et al., 2002; Lachman et al., 1994). However, several scholars do not endorse how many developing countries conduct their reforms. Those late-movers should indeed focus on the domestic application and adaptation of international approaches to survive in fierce global competitions and become less distracted by their competitors' push. Analyzing the rationale of this "borrowing theory," Huntington (1997) took a historical example and denounced latent Western-centralism. As for China's developmental trajectory, he compared the diffusion of Indian Buddhism during the Han Dynasty with the Western-oriented transition after the opening-up in 1979. Ancient China's mainstream value system incorporated Buddhism in its imperial power and met the needs of stability as much as possible, but the "Indianization" of China did not progress further, and Chinese culture remained intact, even reforming the Buddhist rituals and celestial belief systems within indigenous Taoism. Similarly, Huntington believed that Christianity, as a Western religious export, would be absorbed but reshaped in some way that is compatible with the essence of Chinese culture, given the fact that "the Chinese have to date consistently defeated intense Western efforts to Christianize them" (Huntington, 1997). As an influential sinology expert well-versed in Chinese policy and diplomatic affairs, Dr. Henry Kissinger tended to endorse Huntington's perspective that China's path to global economic and political power cannot be arbitrarily attributed to an imitation of the West (Henry, 2011).

3 China's Government Reforms: Goals and Realities

If theory is a guide to practice, has China achieved its pragmatic goals by borrowing foreign reform theories? Most of the existing research on this issue relies on key concepts such as administrative performance, decentralization, fiscal revenue and expenditure, or state capacity.

However, these concepts are difficult to measure and susceptible to interpretation distortions or over-deduction in practice. Therefore, it is difficult for scholars to analyze the actual effect of such reforms.

When it comes to China's reform goals, two words are frequently used: the decentralization of authorities and the structural streamlining of central administrations. Nevertheless, existing research fails to answer adequately whether and to what extent have these two reform goals been achieved. Here we aim to start filling this gap with two groups of first-hand data. The first group concerns the number variation in the Executive Commands of China's State Council and the second group delineates the change of the Council's structure, which is manifested in the overall number of new civil servants employed every year.

What can be learned from the role of the Executive Commands of China's State Council? First, the Council issues Commands of the State Council (CSC), which are of equal status to administrative laws in China, including regulations and decisions and declarations regarding different subjects. Second, it issues Announcements of the State Council (ASC), including suggestions and information about specific public affairs. Third, the State Council releases Reply Letters of the State Council (RLSC), responding to inquiries, requests, and debriefing of provincial governments. CSC, ASC, and RLSC reflect the degree of central government intervention and control over local governments.

As shown in Table 3.2, China's reforms continue to emphasize the implementation of generally more decentralization and practically less

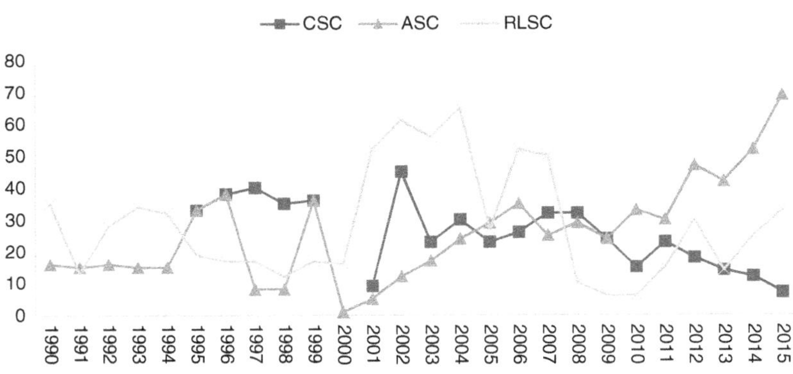

Figure 3.1 The number of CSC, and ASC, and RLSC

Source: Chinese National Council Bulletin, http://sousuo.gov.cn/a.htm?t=bulletin

central governmental interventions. However, Figure 3.1 reveals that the central government's number of interventions and directives usually fluctuates and its numbers have not declined significantly, raising doubts about the actual effects of decentralization efforts. Although it is often difficult to prioritize the importance of CSC, ASC, and RLSC in the administration system, executive commands and orders play a crucial role in China's politics. For instance, local governments still have to ask for the permission of the State Council or central ministries to invest in public infrastructures, such as the high-speed railway. The Fiscal Transfer Payment System has become an important way for the central government to control local governments in recent years. Sometimes, a third or even more than half of a local government's expenditure in some western cities comes from transfers provided by the central government, according to the national statistics.

Another set of graphs depicts a somewhat disguised sectoral setup. The State Council Communiqué clearly shows that there is a lack of quantitative change in the setup of administrative reform departments in each round. As seen in Table 3.3, the number of Ministries and Committees (M&C) has decreased in the past 60 years, but the alternative departments in different forms increased, indicating that the total number of institutes is relatively stable. This phenomenon indicates

Table 3.3 The number of organizations after all previous reforms of the State Council

	Ministries and Committee (M&C)	*Departments directly under the state council (D.D.)*	*Administrative office under the state council (A.O.)*	*Public institutions (P.I.)*	*Total*
1954	35	19	8	\	62
1956	48	24	8	\	70
1959	39	14	6	\	59
1965	49	22	8	\	79
1970	\	\	\	\	32
1975	29	19	4	\	52
1978	37	32	7	\	76
1982	43	14	2	\	59
1988	41	19	6	\	66
1994	40	13	5	11	69
1998	29	17	6	9	61
2003	28	18	4	14	64
2008	27	16	4	17	64
2013	25	17	7	13	62

Note: \ denotes figure-of-the-year unavailable. Figures come from the State Council Communiqués of the corresponding years.

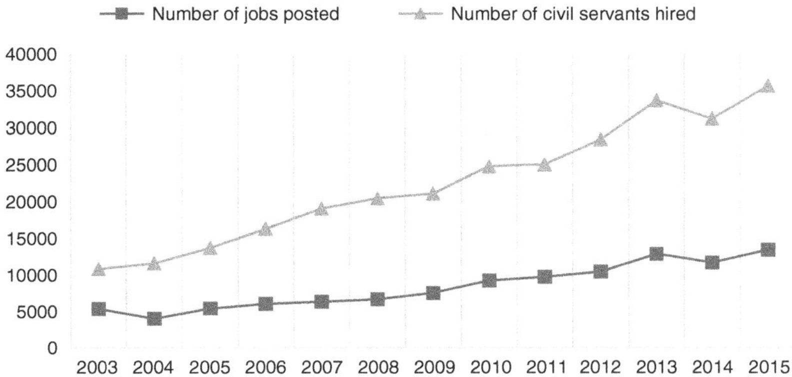

Figure 3.2 The number of jobs posted and the number of civil servants hired in China central government
Source: Chinese National Bureau of Civil Servants

that the dismissed sectors in reform have transformed into other types of departments in China. For example, some central ministries will become state-owned companies in news, media, education, and railway. Therefore, it is argued that the cycle of downsizing and growth during administrative reform has never stopped. There has scarcely been any actual streamlining in government organizations over the past 35 years.

In addition, another concern is that the Chinese government is hiring more and more people. Figure 3.2 shows that the number of new civil servants in China has continued to increase over the past decade. It also suggests that the number of Chinese civil servants has not decreased through the past few reforms.

4 The Complex Adjustment Process between Theories and Practices

The analyses above indicate that China's government reforms have not achieved the expected goals, although China is learning from the experience of western administrative reform. Thus, the following two questions are to be discussed: what makes China's reforms challenging to achieve their goals, and what enlightenment can China's experience and lessons bring to other developing countries?

The most important lesson concerns the danger of ignoring national context when implementing international reform standards in one country. It is widely believed that public management includes a general management model to be applied to different countries. They tended to assume that China had similar conditions and could adopt corresponding reform measures, which proved effective in some Western countries. However, the side effects of such cognitive tendency were less accurate and usually ignored by academics. It may help reduce logical difficulties in comparative research, it also leads to studies divorced from realities and partially affects research outcomes negatively. Chinese scholars are somewhat doctrinally following recommendations proposed by the World Bank and other international organizations. These economic giants happen to maintain a long record of tending to downplay or ignore cultural, historical, and institutional contests among countries when counseling on government reform.

Previous studies have pointed out that differences among countries are objectively complex factors that cannot be wiped away by some "universal" criteria. The potential causality between cultural background and the nature of government was widely discussed in Ruth Benedict's *Patterns of Culture* (1935), Gabriel Almond and Sidney Verba's *The Civic Culture* (1963), as well as Samuel P. Huntington's *The Clash of Civilizations* (1996). Concerns about cultural differences can be traced back to the theories of ancient Greek philosophers (such as Plato and Aristotle), Enlightenment thinkers (such as Rousseau and Montesquieu), as well as modern liberal thinkers. Montesquieu pointed out that

> the political and civil laws of each nation should be the only particular case to which human reason is applied. The law may be applicable to the country where it is made, but it is not necessarily suitable for all countries.
>
> (De Montesquieu, 1989)

This argument was later supported by Robert Dahl, who attributed the interaction between universality and particularity to the keynote issue of "the science of public administration":

> generalizations derived from the operation of public administration in the context of one national-state cannot be universalized and applied to public administration in a different context. A principal may be applicable in a different framework, but its applicability can be determined only after a study of that particular framework.
>
> (Dahl, 1947, p. 2)

Those admonishments, both classical ones and contemporary ones remain vital in guiding administrative reforms. For example, the approach to governmental restructuring currently promoted by the World Bank belittles the differences in cultural backgrounds among countries. It is based on the hypothesis that "even if supranational governance is limited and hampered by divergent traditions, cultures, and political preferences, developing a baseline set of administrative law tools and practices will strengthen whatever supranational policy-making" (Esty, 2006). This research hypothesis has long stoked intense discussions and debates. Moreover, policies associated with the World Bank, IMF, and their donor countries are often criticized by staunch nationalists or protectionists. Thus, such international organizations, in publicity, will weaken the disadvantages and exaggerate the advantages in the concept of governance.

In addition to cultural background differences at the individual and social levels, comparative studies of government reform should not ignore political regime. Each political regime is embedded in a distinctive background providing the *a priori* model for political attitude. The implementation of China's institutional reforms is influenced by the government's internalized socialist theory, encompassing the basic principles of Marxism-Leninism and China's traditional doctrines (e.g., Confucian tenets) on politicking. Ideas or practices that have been proven effective in Western countries have not always had similar effects when blindly implemented in China.

Indeed, despite a gradual convergence toward global standards, China's socialist political system remains unique, and the introduction of foreign administration principles is still challenging. As Joseph Strayer warned, "institutions and beliefs must take root in local soil, or they will wither" (Strayer, 1963).

In the case of China, the most significant difference between China and Western countries is the relationship between the central and local governments, as well as the difference between federalism and unitary state system. Changing socioeconomic circumstances can impact the operation of local government in unique ways to each country. In sum, the structural changes brought by globalization, the evolution in political systems, and demographic variations all play an essential role in government reforms (Andrew & Goldsmith, 1998). Those considerations, however, do not undermine the importance of conducting international comparative research. For example, how to strengthen China's inter-provincial cooperation, and why is it distinctive from America's interstate relationships? What does it take to resolve the intertwined regional conflicts of interest in France? What can we learn from the French experience? Lastly, how can measures be devised to enhance the integration among different governmental levels, thereby avoiding severe confrontation between rural and urban authorities, which has been frequently observed in Southeast Asian nations?

Once a new public administration slogan is established, path dependency makes it relatively stable over a long time. Ideas, regimes (standards), and paradigms derive from political system innovation and result in the formation of ideologies at various stages of institutional innovation. Chinese scholars need to conduct rational indigenous research while making the best use of Chinese and Western cultural input and benefiting from the critical uptake of Western modes of government reforms. Given the analysis as mentioned above, further comments concerning research methods are required.

First, how can we understand the role of theoretical study in government reform? The features of governmental institutions vary in different countries, but a hidden hypothesis is formed in the comparative study; namely, all bureaucratic systems have similar features or will be transformed in the same way. It is particularly apparent among the comparative researchers on reform paradigms. If researchers ignore the differences in the social background between China and other countries, theoretically and practically, this may lead to the misuse and abuse of theories. Due to the arbitrary applications instead of empirical observations and factual descriptions, this kind of research approach can lead to biased conclusions, as criticized by Émile Durkheim: "instead of a science concerned with realities, we produce no more than ideological analysis" (Durkheim, 2014).

The empirical analysis of reforms since China's opening-up concludes as follows: institutional reforms in China were implemented when the priority of all reforms was to suit and serve the needs of economic competitiveness. Unlike institutional reforms in Western countries, China adopted an economic-oriented model: over the past 30 years, the five-yearly governmental reform has always taken place in lockstep with economic reforms. This conformity implies a high degree of correlation and interdependence between the political and economic areas in China. Although the government reform is to promote the development of the market economy, it still contains a lot of ideological factors. Furthermore, China's reforms place greater emphasis on the role of leaders and the Communist Party, while western reforms put more attention on meeting the needs of voters. The difference in emphasis will prevent our research from the risk of devolving into nothing more than "deeply significant nonsense" (Popper, 2012).

Second, how can officials enhance the effectiveness of China's reforms? We have to admit that the Western theories did provide new theoretical tools and examples for developing countries to establish new models of administrative management. However, we should not ignore that Western theories and practices are based on a developed system of information sharing, organizational cooperation, and high quality of government employees, which remains a distant goal for most developing countries. When introducing Western theories and practices, scholars need to consider the reality of imbalanced development stages between North and South. We need to learn more western social-scientific methods to analyze the reforms. For example, when it comes to case studies, the Analytic Hierarchy Process (see Figure 3.3) (AHP), put forward by professor T. L. Saaty, an American operational research expert, has gained popularity among researchers who are struggling in comprehending the labyrinthine and unquantifiable differences among nations (Saaty, 1988). The AHP is a convenient, flexible, and effective multi-criterion decision analysis method notably applicable for the quantitative analysis of qualitative questions. Rather than prescribing a "correct" decision, the AHP helps policy-makers find a solution that suits their goals. It offers a comprehensive and rational framework for structuring the policy-making process and for evaluating alternative solutions.

In China, think tanks are booming nowadays, which can promote the effectiveness of China's reforms. For example, using tools like the AHP, Chinese think tanks could provide alternative policy proposals and evaluate the pros and cons of these policies according to precise standards. In other words, think tanks are the presenters of policy proposals rather than advocates or demonstrators. Government officials need to analyze the characteristics of different policies and then make decisions based on the proposals of think tanks.

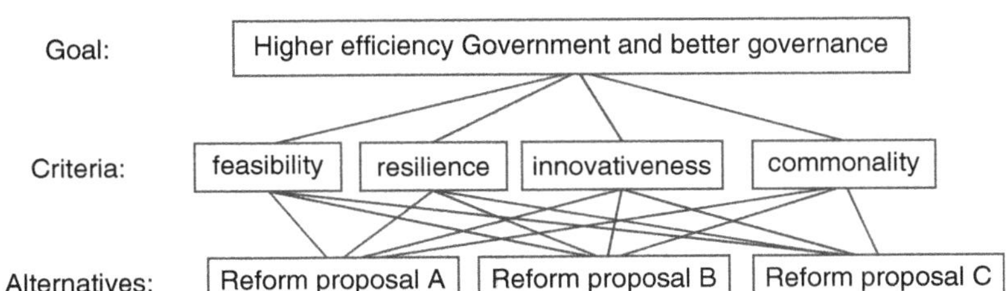

Figure 3.3 The simple Analytic Hierarchy Process model
Source: Authors

5 Conclusion

China's administrative system reforms have drawn lessons from foreign theories and experience, which focused on two aspects: the decentralization of authority and streamlining of the central administration. In this chapter, we consider the backgrounds of countries in the process of policy diffusion and reform knowledge transfer. We hope to avoid the failure and misuse of theoretical transplantation in comparative studies while sharing lessons learned with other developing countries. Of course, we are not trying to overemphasize China's uniqueness or characteristics only to explore universal law's negligence. It has been argued that "incommensurability" between cultures is an obstacle to our understanding of the formation and development of particular political institutions. This is not just an epistemological slogan, but a real dilemma for comparative political studies.

In terms of the three questions we put forward at the beginning, first, the relationships between international theories and China's public administration efforts have been explained. Since the start of reform and opening up in the late 1970s, China has conducted a series of reforms. However, policies in previous reforms looked quite similar to those in Western countries, indicating that imitations might have taken place. Besides, according to Lieberthal (1986), scholars who had been trained in China's mainland could hardly make a difference in the evolution of political science. Therefore, as shown in our research, China's government reforms were not only based on domestic conditions but also had a strong correlation with international practices.

Second, the intended goals set for administrative reforms were a castle in the air in China. Through our analysis, we can see that China has made some achievements in institutional downsizing. For example, the central institutions are getting smaller. However, the effectiveness of decentralization reforms in local areas still needs to be improved, and the central government can still intervene strongly in local affairs. We pointed out that the Chinese government had not achieved the desired reform goals, which does not mean that the reform theory is wrong but that we ignored China's particular background when we borrowed western theories. In addition, the total number of institutions is relatively stable, which is because several ministries and committees have been transformed into other types of institutions, bringing about no change in China's administrative reforms. The number of civil servants has been continuously growing over the last decade, and the State Council has hired more and more officials, which might impair the ongoing streamlining process of the central government. We have made some success in previous reforms, but as for the expected targets, there is still a long way to go.

Third, China's administrative reforms learned from foreign experience and provided insights for similar initiatives in the developing world. The administrative reform itself is a systematic complex, which manifests both Chinese elements and Western fragments. Thus, the greatest challenge for China is to balance the impact of previous Western practices and China's own experience or history. In the era of social, political transformations, one country's experience cannot be absorbed entirely by others due to different contexts. Therefore, the judgment and integration ability of one countries' government officials and think tanks are required for successful reforms, which are expected by other developing countries. Any designs of administrative reforms need to be examined, and their effectiveness should be evaluated by experiments rather than indiscriminate imitations.

To sum up, the best attitude toward Western theories is to be rational, meaning there should be both appreciation and criticism when adopting the theories of western public administrative reforms. In this way, we believe that the government can better carry out the public administration reforms and enhance its competitiveness.

However, there still are some shortcomings in our study due to a variety of reasons, such as insufficient official information, which necessitates more research into this field. For a long time, the public has known almost nothing about the policy-making process of government reforms. It is difficult to find a unique trigger to break the government's monopoly of administrative information. However, we hope that our study can encourage researchers to open the "black box" for even a little.

References

Almond, G. A., & Verba, S. (1963). *The civic culture: Political attitudes and democracy in five nations*. Princeton University Press.

Andrew, C., & Goldsmith, M. (1998). From local government to local governance—and beyond? *International Political Science Review, 19*(2), 101–117.

Andrews, M. (2013). *The limits of institutional reform in development: Changing rules for realistic solutions*. Cambridge University Press.

Askim, J., Christensen, T., Fimreite, A. L., & Lægreid, P. (2009). How to carry out joined-Up government reforms: Lessons from the 2001–2006 Norwegian welfare reform. *International Journal of Public Administration, 32*(12), 1006–1025.

Aufrecht, S. E., & Bun, L. S. (1995). Reform with Chinese characteristics: The context of Chinese civil service reform. *Public Administration Review, 55*, 175–182.

Bhagat, R. S., Kedia, B. L., Harveston, P. D., & Triandis, H. C. (2002). Cultural variations in the cross-border transfer of organizational knowledge: An integrative framework. *Academy of Management Review, 27*(2), 204–221.

Burns, J. P. (2000). Public sector reform and the state: The case of China. *Public Administration Quarterly, 24*, 419–436.

Caulfield, J. L. (2006). The politics of bureau reform in sub-Saharan Africa. *Public Administration and Development, 26*(1), 15–26.

Chan, H. S., & Chow, K. W. (2007). Public management policy and practice in western China: Meta policy, tacit knowledge, and implications for management innovation transfer. *The American Review of Public Administration, 37*(4), 479–498.

Cheung, A. B. L. (1997). Understanding public-sector reforms: Global trends and diverse agendas. *International Review of Administrative Sciences, 63*(4), 435–457.

Christensen, T., Dong, L., Painter, M., & Walker, R. M. (2012). Imitating the West? Evidence on administrative reform from the upper echelons of Chinese Provincial Government. *Public Administration Review, 72*(6), 798–806.

Christensen, T., & Lægreid, P. (2002). *New public management: The transformation of ideas and practice.* Ashgate Pub Limited.

Christensen, T., Lisheng, D., & Painter, M. (2008). Administrative reform in China's central government—How much learning from the West'? *International Review of Administrative Sciences, 74*(3), 351–371.

Dahl, R. A. (1947). The science of public administration: Three problems. *Public Administration Review, 7*(1), 1–11.

De Montesquieu, C. (1989). *Montesquieu: The spirit of the laws.* Cambridge University Press.

Dent, M. (2005). Post-new public management in public sector hospitals? The UK, Germany, and Italy. *Policy & Politics, 33*(4), 623–636.

Dunleavy, P., Margetts, H., Bastow, S., & Tinkler, J. (2006). New public management is dead—Long live digital-era governance. *Journal of Public Administration Research and Theory, 16*(3), 467–494.

Durkheim, E. (2014). *The rules of sociological method: And selected texts on sociology and its method.* Simon and Schuster.

Elias, S. A. (2006). New public management in developing countries: An analysis of success and failure with particular reference to Singapore and Bangladesh. *International Journal of Public Sector Management, 19*(2), 180–203.

Esty, D. C. (2006). Good governance at the supranational scale: Globalizing administrative law. *The Yale Law Journal, 115*, 1490–1562.

Foster, V. (2005). *Ten years of water service reform in Latin America: Toward an Anglo-French model.* Victorian Picturesque the Colonial Gardens of William Sangster.

Gendron, Y. Cooper, D. J., & Townley, B. (2001). In the name of accountability-state auditing, independence, and new public management. *Accounting, Auditing & Accountability Journal, 14*(3), 278–310.

Haque, M. S., & Turner, M. (2013). Knowledge-building in Asian public administration: An introductory overview. *Public Administration and Development, 33*(4), 243–248.

Henry, K. (2011). *On China*. New York, NY: The Penguin Press.

Hood, C. (1991). A public management for all seasons? *Public Administration, 69*(1), 3–19.

Hood, C., & Peters, G. (2004). The middle-aging of new public management: Into the age of paradox? *Journal of Public Administration Research and Theory, 14*(3), 267–282.

Huang, Y. (2008). *Capitalism with Chinese characteristics: Entrepreneurship and the state*. Cambridge: Cambridge University Press.

Huntington, S. P. (1997). *The clash of civilizations and the remaking of world order*. India: Penguin Books.

Kaboolian, L. (1998). The new public management: Challenging the boundaries of the management vs. administration debate. *Public Administration Review, 58*(3), 189–193.

Kim, S., Ashley, S., & Lambright, W. H. (2014). *Public administration in the context of global governance*. Cheltenham: Edward Elgar Publishing.

Lachman, R., Nedd, A., & Hinings, B. (1994). Analyzing cross-national management and organizations: A theoretical framework. *Management Science, 40*(1), 40–55.

Lieberthal, K. (1986). China and political science. *P.S.: Political Science & Politics, 19*(01), 70–78.

Meier, K., Andersen, S. C., O'Toole Jr., L. J., Favero, N., & Winter, S. C. (2015). Taking managerial context seriously: Public management and performance in U.S. and Denmark schools. *International Public Management Journal, 18*(1), 130–150.

Minogue, M., & Polidano, C. (1998). *Beyond the new public management*. Cheltenham: Edward Elgar Publishing.

Ngok, K., & Zhu, G. (2007). Marketization, globalization and administrative reform in China: A zigzag road to a promising future. *International Review of Administrative Sciences, 73*(2), 217–233.

Osborne, D., & Gaebler, T. (1992). *Reinventing government: How the entrepreneurial spirit is transforming government*. Reading, MA: Addison Wesley Public Comp.

Pillay, S. (2008). A cultural ecology of new public management. *International Review of Administrative Sciences, 74*(3), 373–394.

Pollitt, C. (2001). Clarifying convergence. Striking similarities and durable differences in public management reform. *Public Management Review, 3*(4), 471–492.

Pollitt, C., Birchall, J., & Putnam, K. (1998). *Decentralising public sector management*. London: Macmillan.

Popper, K. (2012). *The open society and its enemies*. London: Routledge.

Richard, B., & George, L. (2004). *The changing role of government: The reform of public services in developing countries*. New York: Palgrave Macmillan.

Rothstein, B. (2015). The Chinese paradox of high growth and low quality of government: The cadre organization meets Max Weber. *Governance, 28*(4), 533–548.

Saaty, T. L. (1988). What is the analytic hierarchy process? Mathematical models for decision support. In G. L. Bruce, E. A. Wasil, & P. T. Harker (Eds.), *The analytic hierarchy process: Applications and studies* (pp. 109–121). New York: Springer.

Samaratunge, R., Alam, Q., & Teicher, J. (2008). The new public management reforms in Asia: A comparison of South and Southeast Asian countries. *International Review of Administrative Sciences, 74*(1), 25–46.

Strayer, J. R. (1963). The historical experience of nation-building in Europe. In K. W. Deutsch & W. J. Foltz (Eds.) *Nation building in comparative contexts* (pp. 17–26). London: Routledge.

Su, T-T., Walker, R. M., & Xue, L. (2013). Reform and transition in public administration theory and practice in Greater China. *Public Administration, 91*(2), 253–260.

Waldo, D. (1976). *Comparative and development administration-retrospect and prospect-introductory comments. Public Administration Review, 36*(6), 615–615.

Warner, M. (2008). Reassessing human resource management 'with Chinese characteristics': An overview: Introduction. *The International Journal of Human Resource Management, 19*(5), 771–801.

Weiss, L. (2003). *States in the global economy: Bringing domestic institutions back*. Cambridge: Cambridge University Press.

Welch, E., & Wong, W. (1998). Public administration in a global context: Bridging the gaps of theory and practice between western and non-western nations. *Public Administration Review, 58*, 40–49.

Zhang, C. (2017). How to merge Western theories and Chinese indigenous theories to study Chinese politics? *Journal of Chinese Political Science, 22*(2), 1–12.

4 Political Legitimacy beyond Electoral Democracy

The Crafty Internet Application Strategy in China

1 Introduction

"*The 48th Statistical China's Report on Internet Development*" from the China Internet Network Information Center in 2022 showed that the Internet penetration rate in China had reached 71.6%. With the popularization of Internet and mobile information technology, China's politics, economy, society, and culture have undergone profound changes. For example, 62% of Internet users can access public services information through e-government. The Internet has increased the openness of China's political opportunity structure by creating a more convenient information exchange platform with lower costs and a more active social network for the public (Zheng & Wu, 2005). However, the Internet is often a double-edged sword in practice, both as a powerful tool for public political participation in democratic countries and as a policy leverage for authoritarian governments.

The Internet has also played a complicated role in China. On the one hand, "Internet+" national strategy allows multi-level governance to engage players from multiple levels of governments and multiple sectors for governance results. On the other hand, the Internet censorship hinders the effective dissemination of information, thus affecting the citizen's right to know. In the context that the Internet development was led by its government, it is unlikely to provide adequate support for China's political transition, social integration and value reconstruction (Herold, 2009). Thus, how to analyze the role of the Internet in China's political development remains a puzzle. Moreover, it's still doubted whether the Internet will have a fundamental negative impact on China's political system and political legitimacy.

DOI: 10.4324/9781003363712-4

Scholars from both home and abroad generally believed that the Internet in China, under the control of the information censorship system, can hardly display its "borderless" and "anarchy" features (Xu et al., 2011). But research needs to be conducted to further clarify the following issues: whether the Internet and information technology pose a negative impact on the Chinese government's legitimacy? Is the Chinese government only able to alleviate the legitimacy crisis through suppression and information censorship in the Internet age? This chapter finds that, on the one hand, the Chinese government conducts information censorship on the Internet for the purpose of restriction and penetration, and on the other hand, it also enhances its governance capacity and political legitimacy by actively using the Internet and information technology.

The chapter identifies, conceptualizes, and distinguishes four Internet-based strategies that the Chinese government has adopted to strengthen its legitimacy: responsiveness-driven strategy (RDS), public service and efficiency-oriented strategy (PSEOS), social control orientation strategy (SCOS), and orderly limited participation orientation strategy (OLPOS). Based on the analysis of these four strategies' influence on the government responsiveness, public services, social stability, and the democratic system reform, the authors discuss how the government can resolve the legitimacy crisis and maintain political stability in various ways with the help of the Internet. Meanwhile, the positive effect of the Internet on legitimacy is limited by the quality and penetration level of technology, which means the Internet is far from a foolproof tool and may still lead to potential legitimacy crisis.

The authors first review the debates over the impact of the Internet on the transition of China's polity and its legitimacy; Second, the mechanism and differences in effect of the four strategies are expounded, verified and compared through multiple diachronic cases, including both provincial and nationwide ones. The data are gathered mainly by collating and analysis of government documents and official news reports. Finally, this chapter discusses the relationship among four strategies, and concludes the risks and disadvantages in utilizing technology to strengthen legitimacy. We expand the interpretation of sources of legitimacy in the Internet era within the authoritarian state. Meanwhile, the shaping of China's political resilience and institutional flexibility in the new era has also been further explained.

2 The Impacts of Internet Politics on China's Legitimacy: Research Debates and Interpretation Dilemmas

2.1 Legitimacy and Its Sources

Legitimacy is an important issue in political studies. The implication of legitimacy is considered as people's initiative support and political identification of their regime since John Locke put forward the theory. Some scholars often assume that multi-party election with universal suffrage is the only source of political legitimacy (Beetham, 1991; Berman, 2007; Carothers, 2007). However, the major sources of legitimacy of the authoritarian regime are economic development, achievements of government, ideology, and international environment (Chen, 2005; Schatz, 2006), which lack electoral procedures or democratic institutions.

But, legitimacy is a "mushy concept that political analysts do well to avoid" (Huntington, 1991), its complexity decides that legitimacy has diverse sources in different times and regions. Apart from the election, some scholars argue that legality, justification, consent are also indicators of legitimacy (Gilley, 2006), and the qualities of government, including administrative efficiency, degree of corruption, and discrimination, are more essential than fair election (Rothstein, 2008). Therefore, the sources of legitimacy should be explored from a multidimensional perspective, and it involves at least justice, efficiency, order, democracy, and economy. From these aspects, the authors will discuss the impact of the Internet on the legitimacy of authoritarian states including China.

The rapid development of the Internet has played an important role in global democratization in recent years. For instance, the success of the Arab spring and other color revolutions depended on the support of the Internet (Khondker, 2011). And those events also offered great hopes to the whole world about whether the Internet technology can lead to democratic transitions or the change of legitimacy sources in authoritarian states. Some existing researches believe that the Internet blocking and censorship in authoritarian states will limit its capability in political reform, especially the ability to promote democratic transition (Maerz, 2016). Technologies are neutral. However, they can be used both to promote the public's living standard and restrict people's freedom. As Lakoff and Mesthene (1970) stated, technology creates new possibilities for people's choice and action, but its goals to achieve rest with the preference of technologists. The authors take China as the case to find out how it utilizes technology to prevent the loss of political legitimacy. The ensuing parts will first review the political influence and its debates on the Internet, and then point out the dilemma and misunderstanding of China's Internet politics in extant studies.

Scholars have not yet reached a consensus on the impact of the Internet on the political transformation of authoritarian countries. Some consider Internet communication and social media as key factors in facilitating the new wave of democratization (Farrell, 2012; Howard & Hussain, 2011; Lotan et al., 2011; Tufekci & Wilson, 2012), for the reason that Internet-based media transmits information involving officials' corruption, brutal repression and social injustice with higher speed and lower cost (Diamond, 2010), resulting in collective actions on the Internet as one of the public's way to revolt against authoritarian governments (Rheingold, 2008; Schneier, 2018). Scholars also suggest that the strict information censorship system implemented by countries (e.g. China, Singapore, Iran, and Cuba) made it impossible for open and free Internet environment, as a result, it further enables the government to cultivate a more compliant group of citizens. Furthermore, these countries prefer to view the Internet as an approach for economic growth and technological innovation (Morozov, 2011), rather than a way to increase the public's political consultative capacities or to create diversified information flows (Mercer, 2004; Murphy, 2009).

2.2 China's Legitimacy and Its Debates

The impact of the Internet on China's politics seems to have presented a complicated picture that combines the features of other authoritarian states, and thus the disputes mentioned above can still be seen in each phase of China's Internet development. Some scholars argue that the Internet may promote China's democratization (Zheng, 2007), especially in terms of providing the public with more opportunities to express ideas and influence policy-making. However, the tendency showed that the Internet community weakened the legitimacy of the Communist Party of China as people criticized the government and called for freedom of speech (Esarey & Qiang, 2011), so S. S. Wang and Hong (2010) believed that it is hard for China to form a civil society under its strict Internet censorship. Government's control over the Internet and its cooperation with private Internet enterprises brought constant updates to its information censorship capabilities, transforming China into a more adaptive networked authoritarianism (Tsai, 2016). And Mackinnon (2007) emphasized that the Internet is merely an instrument of political evolution for China, rather than a way for dramatic reforms.

With respect to China's political legitimacy, there are three different standpoints concerning the impact of the Internet: M. Tang and Huhe (2014) suggested that even though China's government has made effective restrictions on access to critical information and sensitive subject, some negative messages are still widely disseminated throughout the Internet. As a result, it will be hard for the government to gain people's support and trust; Stockmann and Gallagher (2018) suggested that China's government is able to reverse the negative impact of social media opinions with its flexible Internet governance strategies, which both offer netizens the freedom of relatively liberal discussion and limit the freedom within the acceptable range of the ruling party. That makes it advantageous for the Communist Party of China to shape the regime legitimacy in the new era (Zuckerman, 2013); However, Hassid (2012), Tong and Zuo (2014) concluded that the impact of the Internet on China's legitimacy varies as the government takes different ways to respond to online public opinions, it should not be simplified as either a reinforcing or a weakening effect.

The authors find that existing researches have painted a complicated picture of the Internet's influence on China's legitimacy, but there are still weaknesses: First, most of the empirical studies are based on cross-sectional data, which can only reflect the difference in the degree of change in legitimacy, but cannot reflect the historical change process. Second, most of these researches took social media as the subject for analysis to infer the growing trend of China's Internet politics. Third, these researches generally criticize the information censorship. They often focus on the contentious game between society and government while neglecting the active adaptability of the government when faced with a legitimate crisis and regional development disparities. In short, extant researches ignored the context of historical and time dimension. Lynch (2011) pointed out that despite the democratic nature of the Internet, its capability to weaken the information control of authoritarian states cannot be accurately predicted in the short term. Meanwhile, there is no fixed connection between the Internet and political output. Thus, the authors find it necessary to analyze the level of China's political legitimacy from a more comprehensive, objective, and rational perspective.

3 Strategies of Enhancing Political Legitimacy in China's Internet Era

3.1 Political Legitimacy in China's Internet Era

Since the reform and opening up, economic performance, especially continuous high growth, has been the most important support for the Chinese government's legitimacy (Schubert, 2008; White, 2005). However, China's complex political context leaves space for a certain degree of political freedom and democracy, providing the government with a diversified source of legitimacy. For example, due to the lack of a competitive electoral system in China, the government has adopted various consultation mechanisms and set up villager self-governance, policy hearings, etc., to gather public opinion. This is also known as "consultative authoritarianism" (Lieberthal & Lampton, 1992; Teets, 2013).

Some scholars have found that China's policy-makers are not only limited to officials within the system, but more and more NGOs, media, and think tanks are participating in policy-making, showing the characteristics of "fragmented authoritarianism 2.0" (Mertha, 2009). Therefore, China explores multiple sources of government legitimacy beyond government performance and economic growth. In addition, the improvement of administrative performance has prompted the government to pay more attention to the rationality and efficiency of governance.

So, in China, political legitimacy not only roots in election, but also comes from government efficiency, government transparency, and social order. The Internet technology has given the CPC opportunities and ability to influence these dimensions through e-government and "Internet+ public service". Is the Internet weakening or strengthening the Chinese government's political legitimacy today? To answer this question, the authors concluded four strategies the Chinese government adopted with regard to Internet technology, and demonstrates, through case studies, how the Internet shapes Chinese government's legitimacy by intervening in different dimensions.

In general, the advantage of a case study lies in that it can verify and develop theories by using observational data. But the selection bias or less rigorous study design will result in a subjective conclusion. Thus, whether the cases selected feature enough representativeness or not is vital to reflecting the causality. Flyvbjerg (2006) regarded specific context-dependent cases as the basis of theoretical induction. Seawright and Gerring (2008) classified cases into four categories: typical case, diverse case, extreme case and deviant case, among which the typical case features the most representativeness. Another research further pointed out that the choice of small sample cases must follow the goal-driven principle (which is non-stochastic) (Box-Steffensmeier et al., 2008). Based on these guidelines, this chapter selected four typical cases, taking the diffusion scope and effect as the standards, ensuring the cases' high representativeness in demonstrating Chinese government's strategies.

3.2 Four Strategies to Improve Political Legitimacy in China

The authors divide Chinese legitimacy construction strategies into the following four types:

The first is RDS (Responsiveness-driven Strategy). The authors start with "letters and visits" system (信访*XinFang*, complaint and petition). As both the most direct communication channel between citizens and the government. The authors chose the "Sunshine Petition Online System" in Huai'an City, Jiangsu Province. It is the model of China's Internet letters and visits system, which has been promoted among two thirds of China's local governments.

The second is PSEOS (Public Service and Efficiency Orientation Strategy). This chapter takes e-government as an example. With China's e-government gradually transforming from merely serving the government to serving the public, increasing numbers of public services are required to be accessible online. It is a symbol that the government is attempting to improve its efficiency through technology. Among many local authorities, Zhejiang Province plays a leading role in China in building the government's website. And its achievement in reform was praised in the State Council's *Report on the Work of the Government* and became a model for other provinces.

The third is the SCOS (Social Control Orientation Strategy). The authors choose the Internet monitoring system as an example. The *Tianyan* detection and monitoring system utilizes 20 million network-connected cameras, covering nearly all cities in China, to maintain social order and security. As one of the most important social regulation instruments in China, it embodies the level of social control of the Chinese government.

The Fourth is OLPOS (Orderly Limited Participation Orientation Strategy). This chapter takes the online public consultation system as an example. Since 2005, this system has been the most important Internet-based channel for the public to participate in decision-making in China. Meanwhile, the reform of online car-hailing service is a joint effort made by the government and the whole society, which witnessed extensive use of Internet tools by both local and central governments. The event displayed both the tolerance and inherent limitations of online public consultation systems regarding public engagement. All of these will be fully illustrated in the following parts.

4 Strategy 1: Responsiveness-Driven Strategy (RDS)

China's rapid economic growth has also brought about negative impacts such as inequality and bureaucratic corruption (Holbig & Gilley, 2010; Zeng, 2014). China's petitioning system has always been the main channel for the public to practice their appealing rights, and for the government to defuse social pressure. It also helps officials in shaping their image of "servants-of-the-people". However, petitioning through traditional ways such as telephone calls, letters, or visits, due to their inefficiency, cannot meet people's great demand. More and more people abandon the formal system and choose to make their complaints heard through collective and radical protests (O'Brien, 2008). Under the predicament of coercion and bribery, coupled with the unwillingness of petitioning groups to communicate peacefully, China has long been inefficient in responding to social pressure (J. Wang, 2015). This fragile informal political interaction not only weakens the legitimacy and justice of local governments but also erodes the political trust of the central government.

However, the Internet technology makes it possible for the government to establish a more effective social response mechanism. For example, China's governments at all levels have set up extensive online complaint platforms as more convenient, orderly and low-cost complaints channel for the public. At the same time, through the analysis of big data on social petition information, the government has given priority to reshaping the procedures of policy-making & supervision, and solving the most prominent problems in social development. Although fairness cannot be adequately guaranteed, this mechanism provides the Chinese government with the potential to enhance justice by setting up a series of stable processes.

W. Tang (2016) argues that China's paternalistic governance makes it lack public responsiveness. Once the government becomes more responsive, it will be easy to gain public support and trust, and the relationship between the government and society will also be improved. The improvement of response efficiency demonstrates the achievements of Internet-based technology. It provided the CPC with new tools to ease the social pressure and shape its positive image among the people to obtain legitimacy.

The authors take the building of online petitioning system of Huai'an City, Jiangsu Province from 2007 to 2016 as an example, in an effort to explain how the Internet technology can be adopted to improve government response.

Case 1: Huai'an "Sunshine Petition" Story

Huai'an is located in the eastern coastal province of Jiangsu, with a total GDP of $53 billion and a per capita GDP of $10,235 in 2017, ranking 11th in the province. However, with the agricultural and industrial sectors accounting for more than half of its GDP, there is still a large floating population and low-income groups. Therefore, the society of Huai'an has always had all kinds of fierce conflicts.

In this context, Huai'an began to develop the "Sunshine Petitioning Online System" independently and implemented it in January, 2007. The main function of the system is to use the Internet and big data to handle the citizen's petition activities comprehensively. There are three significant differences between Huai'an's system and the traditional ones. First, the "Sunshine Petitioning Online System" combines registration and duplicate elimination of the offline and online petition data to ensure that public appeals can be fully reflected in the government's database. Second, it can carry out classified communication and dynamic monitoring of registered petitions by dividing the responding time into "within 15 days", "within 45 days", "within 60 days" and "more than 60 days", which also serves as a reminder for government departments to respond in a timely manner. Third, based on the data of petitions, the system has established two evaluation indexes, the "Comprehensive Petitioning Index" and the "Petition Handling Satisfaction Index", to evaluate the level of local social stability and performance of departments.

Until 2013, Huai'an had included nine counties (districts), 147 townships (streets) and more than 400 government departments in its "Sunshine Petitioning Online System", producing a series of positive results, with online petitions accounting for 49% of the total, the rate of one-off settlement of petitions reaching

86%, and the proportion of repeated petitions dropping to 9%. In particular, the average processing time of government-related petitions had been shortened from 45 days to 33 days,[1] and the total amount of petitions had been decreasing for seven consecutive years. Based on these positive results, the "Sunshine Petitioning Online System" has attracted the attention of the central government, which calls on other cities to learn from Huai'an's experience.

At the national level, online petitions accounted for 43.6% of the total in 2015. Provincial online petitions accounted for over 50% of the total,[2] and the total number of petitions in 2016 dropped by 23% compared with that of 2013.[3] Although it is not clear whether the online petitioning has improved China's social and political stability, these achievements still show that a growing number of demands for impartiality could be addressed and met through online platforms.

Of course, this case is only one of the ways in which the petition situation has been improved. Governments at all levels have also explored a variety of Internet-based responding mechanisms as a supplement to existing petitioning channels, such as "online message board for local government officials" on people.com, which has been in use since 2006. And, the "political forum" built by local governments also shoulders the responsibility of listening and responding to public opinions.

5 Strategy 2: Public Service and Efficiency Orientation Strategy (PSEOS)

While RDS focuses on leveraging technology to improve the government's ability to address the needs of vulnerable groups and social conflicts, governments remain passive in legitimacy. In addition, public policy often lags behind the occurrence and evolution of social conflicts. Cadres should focus on issues such as public service and government efficiency to reduce social pressure, for certain situations such as low administrative efficiency, red tape process, administrative bulwark, rent-setting and rent-seeking still exist in China's government, tending to cause "local legitimacy deficits" (Li, 2013).

In fact, China's government is exploiting Internet technology to make it easier to provide more accessible public service, more efficient administrative procedures, and more transparent operations. All of these can contribute to legitimacy. E-government building in recent years may be a good example. This chapter names the related actions as Public Service and Efficiency Orientation Strategy (PSEOS).

Specifically, on the one hand, Internet technology can break administrative barriers among different government departments so as to realize the integration and sharing of administrative resources within the system. Furthermore, it can also save the administrative costs and improve the administrative efficiency for governments. On the other hand, enhanced government effectiveness also creates more accessible public services. By adopting Internet technologies, the gap between the quality of government services and commercial services has been narrowing down in a continuous way. As more and more apps for public services being launched by governments at different levels, China might turn into a state of "Internet consultative authoritarianism".

Faced with social discontent and international disputes caused by Internet censorship, the Chinese government makes use of the Internet technology to improve service and performance, which are good supplements to legitimacy. Maerz (2016) initiated an empirical study of authoritarian countries such as Russia, Kazakhstan, and Turkmenistan, and found that e-government is an effective tool for acquiring public support. Similarly, Oliver (2014) argued that, to a great extent, the success of the government democracy is related to the country's public service performance. Therefore, China's investment in e-government will be helpful in maintaining its legitimacy in the long-term.

The following is a study on the e-government development of Zhejiang Province, a relatively more developed eastern province in China, from the year of 2014 to 2017. The study gives specific interpretation to the enhancement of government effectiveness and legitimacy.

Case 2: The Story of the Establishment of Zhejiang Government Service Website

Zhejiang Province is located in the southeastern part of China, a more developed region in terms of economy. The total GDP of this province in 2017 registered 780.8 billion U.S. dollars, equaling the world's 11th economy—the Netherlands. E-commerce (such as Alibaba) and other Internet industries within the province already made eye-catching achievements, creating a friendly environment for the development of Internet technology.

Since 2013, Zhejiang Province started to build a government service network that integrates various public services. Compared with the traditional administrative process, the advantages of online services are mainly shown in three aspects. First, the public can apply for services online. The Internet service platform can provide the public with open and transparent government information inquiry and quick and orderly administrative licensing, administrative punishment, etc. Second, departments share information online, integrating the data from some 100 cities and 1,350 towns by adopting cloud platforms and big data technology. Third, online services help simplify the process and cut administrative costs. A inter-department online administrative processing, auditing and approving platform for a variety of issues has been established, making it possible for one-stop online application and approval across multiple departments. It saves both physical efforts and time cost for examination and approval.

By the end of 2017, the number of registered users of Zhejiang government service network has totaled more than 14 million, computer-terminal visits reached more than 900 million, and the number of available online administrative services increased to more than 80,000. For example, a total number of 1.35 million applications for industrial and commercial registration were received, in which 1.12 million were processed. And the number of handled payment services reached 32.08 million, with a total amount of 15.5 billion yuan.

Apart from Zhejiang Province, China currently has a total of 47,941 government websites and 134,827 government social media accounts. The number of online government service users has reached 485 million, accounting for 62.9% of all Internet users. A city service platform was also established on the basis of an instant messaging service app—WeChat, and it has attracted 417 million users.[4] Meanwhile, 69 cities in China have launched a total of 316 mobile government services apps.

6 Strategy 3: Social Control Orientation Strategy (SCOS)

It can be seen in the third wave of democratization that ineffective government is the cause of the collapse of many emerging democracies and then the return of authoritarianism. China has always been employing a stable bureaucratic system and administrative performance to maintain the effectiveness of the governance. However, its social governance capacity has long been impaired by the large population base, the gap between the rich and the poor, and the complex population mobility, etc. In order to get rid of this dilemma, on the one hand, the Chinese government is continuously expanding its fiscal spending on social security while implementing many campaign-style governance performances, which may only be effective in the short term. On the other hand, it can also choose to use the Internet and other advanced technologies to improve enforcement ability, and strives to build an efficient social control system.

Internet technology can bring about an unparalleled impact on social control. It is also an advantageous tool for the Chinese government who emphasizes social stability and order. The following part will be explained with the case of the *Tianyan* detection and monitoring system.

Case 3: The Story of *Tianyan* Detection and Monitoring System

The Internet and information technology have been constantly applied to the field of social security management since China promoted the strategies of "safety city" and "police with science and technology" in 2004. The most fundamental achievement is the *Tianyan* detection and monitoring system based on big data and cloud storage. The government has installed a large number of Internet-connected cameras in every street and corner of the city to grant security departments real-time remote supervision and control. For instance, it can record and track traffic violations, criminal activities, suspects at large and emergencies, etc.

Tianyan detection system relies on dynamic face recognition technology, which can accurately recognize more than 40 kinds of face features. It can accurately recognize faces according to different perspectives, light and shade differences, dynamic and static conditions, etc. In addition, the speed of this system is amazing. To be specific, it can compare 3 billion times per second, and takes one second to "screen" the national population and two seconds to "screen" the world population. The accuracy of dynamic Tianyan detection is also very high. At present, the 1:1 recognition accuracy has reached more than

99.8%, while the human eye recognition accuracy is 97.52%. In China, the government currently adopts this technology to strengthen their governance capacity, which can be reflected by some examples: Guangdong province has set up 920,000 cameras and has solved more than 30,000 cases with the help of the system[5]; the city of Qingdao has tracked down criminals of 6,300 cases in 2013 using *Tianyan*, reaching 40% of the total cases in the whole year.[6] The city of Wuhan had installed 1 million cameras connected with the Internet by the end of 2017, and the number of robbery cases was reduced by 50% every year since 2012.[7] Furthermore, some cities with high economic development levels, such as Beijing, Shanghai, Shenzhen, Ningbo, have already been using facial recognition and sonar positioning technologies in the *Tianyan* detection and monitoring system. In these cities, real-time snapshot and ID recognition can be used on regulation-violating pedestrians and vehicles, the fine can then be paid online.

7 Strategy 4: Orderly Limited Participation Orientation Strategy (OLPOS)

Systems such as the People's Congress, Political Consultative Conference and Grassroots Democratic Elections, which provide opportunities for social elites and leaders to participate in political affairs, are the supplements to less-advanced democracy. However, in the Internet age, the deficiencies of the socialist democratic system in terms of independence, representation and negotiation are more exposed. At the same time, with the growth of middle class, the willingness and decision-making ability of the public to participate in political affairs has also improved.

At present, the Internet is crucial to political participation and democracy in China. For example, departments openly solicit opinions through the Internet and establish a system of orderly but limited participation. The government uses the Internet to publish the first draft of the policy to solicit public opinion and lay the foundation for rational decision-making. But gathering public opinion online has little to do with regime change. Instead, it could be a technical complement to non-competitive elections. The author takes the regulatory reform of China's online taxi-hailing service from 2013 to 2016 as an example to illustrate the impact of online public opinion collection.

Case 4: Regulation Reform of Online Taxi-Hailing Service

Since 2010, online taxi-hailing service gradually became a booming business in more than 300 cities across the country within just four years.[8] Private cars accounted for a large proportion of online taxi-hailing service. They charge low prices while providing customers with a more convenient service because car owners don't have to pay taxi contract fees and taxes. But it also brought negative effects: the government's management pressure on the taxi industry; negative impact on the market order of the traditional taxi industry, and challenges to the monopoly position of taxi companies.

In the early stage, there were government's approval but a lack of regulations on online taxi-hailing business, resulting in discontent from traditional taxi industries. Then, the society witnessed strong opposition among the taxi drivers and operators in a form of strike or demonstrations in cities such as Nan Jing, Chang Chun, Ji Nan. Furthermore, other local governments (such as those of Shen Zhen, Su Zhou, Shen Yang, etc.) banned online taxi -hailing services, but were then criticized by local users on the Internet.

To better manage app-based ride-hailing services, some local governments have adjusted their policies by collecting public comments on government websites. Other cities collect opinions through official websites, government mailboxes, etc. In Wuhan, Kunming, Hangzhou as well as other cities, the related policies were adjusted, gaining the public's support and praises in media and on Internet forums.

Through the online public opinions system on the website of the Legal Office of the State Council, the Ministry of Transportation also sought support for the decision about online taxi-hailing service in October 2015. The Ministry has received 5,008 valid opinions online in just one month. They were then divided into 6,832 specific opinions, among which more than 70% were in favor of the legalization of online car-hailing services.[9] But the specific suggestions adopted are decided by the Ministry of Transportation.

Besides, the online opinions-gathering system at the central-government level has been used more frequently. From 2005 to 2017, the number of draft laws published on the Internet has reached 133, showing a generally upward trend. The number of draft administrative regulations posted online has reached 207, with an annual average of 18 (see Figure 4.1). Needless to say, this increase is closely related to the progress of the government's reform and the number of new momentous social problems emerged every year, but the online opinions system gradually became a norm. Up to 2017, 130 online taxi-hailing business platforms have launched their own services, and 19 online taxi-hailing business platform companies, such as Shenzhou Special Car, have obtained business licenses, which shows that the effect of the Regulation reform of online taxi-hailing service is obvious.

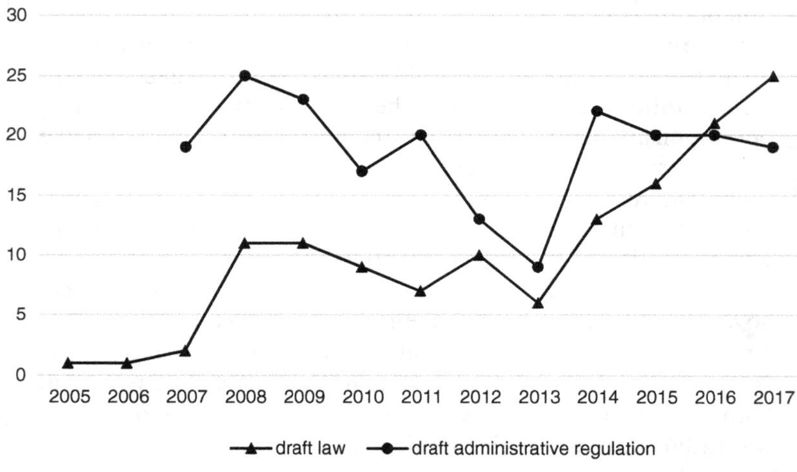

Figure 4.1 The number of draft laws and draft administrative regulations posted for opinions online (2005–2017)

Source: The data were collected from http://www.npc.gov.cn/npc/flcazqyj/node_8195.htm; http://zqyj.chinalaw.gov.cn/overCollectionList?draftType=1.

8 Discussion

According to these cases, the authors can conclude that the Internet doesn't necessarily play negative roles in the political legitimacy in China. The Chinese government doesn't only use forcible repression or information censorship to maintain its legitimacy. Instead, it takes advantage of the Internet to set up a series of strategies to mitigate legitimacy crisis. In general, RDS utilizes the Internet response mechanism to provide a more efficient solution to justice problems between government and society. Adopting the platform of e-government,

PSEOS creates a comprehensive public service system to prompt the government to pay more attention to administrative efficiency and transparency. SCOS uses advanced social control technologies, especially the Internet monitoring system, to restrict citizens' behaviors which may undermine social order and public security. OLPOS promotes the legality and democracy of China from a legislative way by establishing a universal online policy-making participation system.

It seems that the four strategies are adopted separately. In fact, there are interactions and mutual transformation among them. First, the public service e-government includes more and more responsive characteristics which originally belongs to the petition system, indicating that RDS is integrated into PSEOS. For example, the main function of government Weibo (Chinese twitter) is to disseminate information, but actual practice shows that governments can also respond to netizens who report against government officials on Weibo. From this perspective, PSEOS may undertake more complex responsibilities so as to reduce the pressure of RDS.

Second, RDS complements OLPOS and may convert to OLPOS under certain conditions. Specifically, the government prefers to adopt RDS when the contradictions and dissensions arise from individuals or small groups, because such problems usually do not necessitate policy adjustment or regulation reform. However, RDS is ineffective when facing large-scale public problems that require extensive responses from the government, so the draft resolutions formed through OLPOS are equivalent to central government's responses to public demands.

Third, some functions of SCOS are integrated into PSEOS. For example, people can query traffic violations recorded by the Internet monitoring system and pay fines through mobile government apps. Through public service platforms, citizens can also acquire the data of road conditions collected by the Internet monitoring system.

The four strategies do not always contribute positively to the government's legitimacy. On the one hand, the penetration rate of Internet technologies depends on economic development and political support. However, the economic resources of eastern, central, and western China are very unbalanced. It will take a long time to implement these strategies nationwide. On the other hand, the quality of information and the way in which they are used have a profound impact on legitimacy. In addition, different strategies have the following shortcomings:

First, in terms of RDS, China's online petition system doesn't include an online processing mechanism, which means the complaining and processing are separate, leading to possible prevarication from the petition department.

Second, in the PSEOS, there are various defects in numerous apps for government services, for instance, the small number of downloads, poor utilization rate, slow update frequency, insignificant functions and essential data missing/deficiency. Some civil servants even began to complain that their self-developed software as "useless in solving problems". Furthermore, the number of official Weibo set by the government is increasing year by year, impairing their original intentions to facilitate political communication, improve government information transparency and provide convenient service for the public.[10] People see little original content, much rigmarole service information, insufficient interaction ability and limited propagation. All of these defects bring no enhancement to the government capacity, adding the risk of being criticized as new "vanity or trophy projects" in the technological age.

Third, it is still in dispute whether the Internet video monitoring system around the cities will undermine individuals' privacy or improve public security. However, to expand the department's authority, law enforcers may abuse or misuse the technology.

Fourth, the Internet has provided more channels for public political participation. However, neither the Internet infrastructure nor the institutions are perfect, which, in turn, may reduce the government's credibility. What's more, the Internet security is one of the heated topics these years. A series of recent events, for example, the disclosure of Prism plan and the scandal that 50 million Facebook users' information were used to manipulate US election, have put the vulnerability of personal privacy under spotlight. According to the statistics released by the Chinese Internet company 360, in 2018, 87.2% of the Chinese government websites and 93.3% of the public institution websites were found to have loopholes for 4.559 million times and 920,000 times respectively.[11] Obviously, the Chinese government had serious security risks when utilizing information technology. Failure to protect public information from security risks will lead to a more unpredictable crisis of legitimacy.

Different strategies reflect diverse characteristics of the initiative and positive effects of the legitimacy. There are multiple restrictive factors in the legitimacy technology strategy of the Chinese government. To thoroughly elaborate on how Internet technology serves the Chinese government, the authors further summarized the differences and relationships among four strategies (see Table 4.1).

Table 4.1 Differences of China's legitimacy strategies in the Internet era

	RDS	*PSEOS*	*SCOS*	*OLPOS*
Cases	Internet petition, discussing policies on forums	Government website, government Weibo, mobile government client applications	"Tianyan" monitoring system	The proposed act posted on the Internet for public comment
The characteristics of government actions	To expand the response scope, improve the response efficiency, and focus on the response result	To break down the administrative barriers and enhance the administrative efficiency and service quality	To strengthen the management intelligence and improve the management accuracy	To widen channels for public political participation and rationalize and democratize decision-making
Feedback from the public	To be easier to get attention and response from the government	To reduce cost of service and obtain convenient service	Restrained illegal behaviors and ascendant self-discipline	Access to political participation
Influence factors of legitimacy	Government response ability, the relations between the government and the society, regime stability	Government service capacity, the relations between the government and the society, government transparency	Government management ability, social order and stability	Democratic system construction
Influence factors of self-quality	Scope of response	The feasibility of functions, the frequency of maintenance and updates	Protection of citizen's privacy	Transparency of opinion processing, the governance efficacy of participants
The relationships between each other	Being absorbed by PSEOS, converting to OLPOS under certain conditions	Reducing the pressure for RDS, cooperating with SCOS	Cooperating with PSEOS	Undertaking the duties of RDS when public problems arise

9 Conclusion

In China, the adoption of the Internet technologies in governance has shown the benefits of opening up the channels for democratic participation and government information transparency. Besides, it also provides governments with tools to tighten and reinforce social control. This chapter summarizes the four strategies of Internet application in Chinese politics, which clearly illustrates the key reasons why China can still maintain strong government resilience and high institutional flexibility in the Internet age.

In fact, China is not the only country taking advantage of these strategies. There are similar approaches to enhance legitimacy in some democratic countries and authoritarian countries. For instance, the White House website set up a section named "Open for Question" in 2011, where users could nominate some important questions to vote and get responses from the government (Fung et al., 2013), like the conjunction of RDS and OLPOS. The Brazilian city of Belo Horizonte initiated an e-participatory budgeting program in 2006, citizens who participated in it could discuss and allocate the financial funds collectively (Peixoto, 2008). What's more, Kyrgyzstan, Kazakhstan, and Uzbekistan are also offering a series of public services through national-level e-government sites. Johnson (2010) believes that these are their performances aiming to strengthen the positive image and legitimacy of regimes.

However, from the analysis on the limiting factors of different strategies, we can see that the Internet and technology are not so powerful as to take the place of public opinion mechanisms such as competitive election and equal consultation. Without considering the human values and historical and cultural background, technology can merely be a supplementary tool to political activity (West, 2010). Thus, this chapter summarizes four strategies for legitimacy enhancement, in order to provide the theoretical and empirical support for understanding the distortions of the technology neutrality in different political backgrounds, which may contribute to a more comprehensive understanding of multiple roles of the Internet in China. All conceptual summaries and case studies, inevitably, have their limitations, such as case selection bias. Looking at the global picture, especially in certain authoritarian states, whether these four types of strategies are applicable still requires rigorous examination with abundant data.

Notes

1 "Sunshine Petitioning Online System" of Huaian: the number of petitions decreased and satisfaction level enhanced for seven years' of

running, people.com.cn reported [EB/OL]. http://politics.people.com.cn/n/2014/0414/c383447–24892599.html. Access time: 2018.4.14.
2 State Bureau for Letters and Calls: online petition account for 43.6% of the total, people.com.cn reported [EB/OL]. http://politics.people.com.cn/n/2015/0629/c1001–27221476.html. Access time: 2018.4.14.
3 National conference on letters and visits: create an online petition service platform that benefits citizens, xinhuanet.com reported [EB/OL]. http://www.xinhuanet.com/politics/2017-07/21/c_129660516.htm. Access time: 2018.4.14.
4 The 41st Statistical Report on Internet Development in China was published on [EB/OL]. http://cnnic.cn/gywm/xwzx/rdxw/201801/t2018013170188.htm. Access time: 2018.4.14.
5 574,000 "Tianyan" detection and monitoring system cameras help police to find criminals, xinhuanet.com reported [EB/OL]. http://www.xinhuanet.com/city/2017-03/02/c_129498868.htm. Access time: 2018.4.14.
6 6000 criminal cases has been broken with the help of "Tianyan" detection and monitoring system, Netease news reported [EB/OL]. http://news.163.com/14/0501/00/9R4B4LLH00014AED.html. Access time: 2018.4.14.
7 Millions of "Tianyan" dection and monitoring system cameras help to build Wuhan's safety net, xinhuanet.com reported [EB/OL]. http://www.hb.xinhuanet.com/2018-04/02/c_1122623968.htm. Access time: 2018.4.14.
8 Didi's chauffeur service accounts for 80% of online car hailing business, xinhuanet.com reported [EB/OL]. http://www.xinhuanet.com/tech/2016-03/02/c_128767312.htm. Access time: 2018.4.14.
9 The Ministry of Transport announced the condition of public opinions collection, xinhuanet.com reported [EB/OL]. http://www.xinhuanet.com/fortune/2015-10/27/c_128361927.htm. Access time: 2018.4.14.
10 Regulation of low efficient government app is urgent, xinhuanet.com reported [EB/OL]. http://www.xinhuanet.com/yuqing/2018-02/12/c_129811571.htm. Access time: 2018.4.14.
11 The 2017 Report on Security Situation of China's Website, 360 Internet Security Center reported [EB/OL]. http://zt.360.cn/1101061855.php?dtid=1101062368&did=490995546. Access time: 2018.4.14.

References

Beetham, D. (1991). *The legitimation of power.* London: Macmillan.
Berman, S. (2007). How democracies emerge: Lessons from Europe. *Journal of Democracy, 18*(1), 28–41.
Box-Steffensmeier, J. M., Brady, H. E., & Collier, D. (2008). *The Oxford handbook of political methodology.* Oxford University Press.
Carothers, T. (2007). How democracies emerge: The "sequencing" fallacy. *Journal of Democracy, 18*(1), 12–28.
Chen, C. (2005). Institutional legitimacy of an authoritarian state: China in the mirror of Eastern Europe. *Problems of Post-Communism, 52*(4), 3–13.
Diamond, L. (Ed.). (2010).*Democratization in Africa: Progress and retreat.* Baltimore, MD: The Johns Hopkins University Press.
Esarey, A., & Qiang, X. (2011). Digital communication and political change in China. *International Journal of Communication, 5*(5), 298–319.

Farrell, H. (2012). The consequences of the Internet for politics. *Annual Review of Political Science, 15*(1), 35–52.

Flyvbjerg, B. (2006). Five misunderstandings about case-study research. *Qualitative Inquiry, 12*(2), 219–245. doi:10.1177/1077800405284363

Fung, A., Gilman, H. R., & Shkabatur, J. (2013). Six models for the internet + politics. *Social Science Electronic Publishing, 15*(1), 30–47.

Gilley, B. (2006). The meaning and measure of state legitimacy: Results for 72 countries. *European Journal of Political Research, 45*(3), 499–525.

Hassid, J. (2012). Safety valve or pressure cooker? Blogs in Chinese political life. *Journal of Communication, 62*(2), 212–230.

Herold, D. K. (2009). Cultural politics and political culture of Web 2.0 in Asia. *Knowledge Technology & Policy, 22*(2), 89–94.

Holbig, H., & Gilley, B. (2010). Reclaiming legitimacy in China. *Politics & Policy, 38*(3), 395–422.

Howard, P. N., & Hussain, M. M. (2011). The role of digital media. *Journal of Democracy, 22*(3), 35–48.

Huntington, S. (1991). *The third wave: Democratization in the late twentieth century.* Norman: University of Oklahoma Press.

Johnson, E. (2010). E-government in authoritarian states: Content analysis of e-government websites in central Asia. *Social Science Electronic Publishing, (2)*, 221–229.

Khondker, H. H. (2011). Role of the new media in the Arab spring. *Globalizations, 8*(5), 675–679.

Lakoff, S. A., & Mesthene, E. G. (1970). Technological change: Its impact on man and society. *Journal of Interdisciplinary History, 2*(4), 490.

Li, L. (2013). The magnitude and resilience of trust in the center: Evidence from interviews with petitioners in Beijing and a local survey in rural China. *Modern China, 39*(1), 3–36.

Lieberthal, K., & Lampton, D. M. (1992). *Bureaucracy, politics, and decision making in post-Mao China.* University of California Press.

Lotan, G., Graeff, E., Ananny, M., Gaffney, D., Pearce, I., & Boyd, D. (2011). The revolutions were tweeted: Information flows during the 2011 Tunisian and Egyptian revolutions. *International Journal of Communication, 5*(5), 1375–1405.

Lynch, M. (2011). After Egypt: The limits and promise of online challenges to the authoritarian Arab State. *Perspectives on Politics, 9*(2), 301–310.

Mackinnon, R. (2007). Flatter world and thicker walls? Blogs, censorship and civic discourse in China. *Public Choice, 134*(1), 31–46.

Maerz, S. F. (2016). The electronic face of authoritarianism: E-government as a tool for gaining legitimacy in competitive and non-competitive regimes. *Government Information Quarterly.*

Mercer, C. (2004). Engineering civil society: ICT in Tanzania. *Review of African Political Economy, 31*(99), 49–64.

Mertha, A. (2009). "Fragmented authoritarianism 2.0": Political pluralization in the Chinese policy process. *China Quarterly, 200*(200), 995–1012.

Morozov, E. (2011). Whither Internet control. *Journal of Democracy, 22*(2), 62–74.

Murphy, E. C. (2009). Theorizing ICTs in the Arab World: Informational capitalism and the public sphere. *International Studies Quarterly, 53*(4), 1131–1153.

O'Brien, K. J. (2008). *Popular protest in China.* Boston: Harvard University Press.

Oliver, A. (2014). Are Australians disenchanted with democracy. *Papers on Parliament, 62.*

Peixoto, T. (2008). *E-participatory budgeting: E-democracy from theory to success?* Social Science Electronic Publishing.

Rheingold, H. (2008). *Using participatory media and public voice to encourage civic engagement.* In W. L. Bennett, D. John, & T. Catherine (Eds.), *Civic life online: Learning how digital media can engage youth* (pp. 97–118). Edited by Cambridge, MA: The MIT Press, 2008.

Rothstein, B. (2008). Creating political legitimacy. *American Behavioral Scientist, 53*, 311–330.

Seawright, J., & Gerring, J. (2008). Case selection techniques in case study research: A menu of qualitative and quantitative options. *Political research quarterly, 61*(2), 294–308.

Schatz, E. (2006). Access by accident: Legitimacy claims and democracy promotion in authoritarian Central Asia. *International Political Science Review, 27*(3), 263–284.

Schneier, B. (2018). On cybersecurity. *Journal of International Affairs, 71*(2), 121–124.

Schubert, G. (2008). One-party rule and the question of legitimacy in contemporary China: Preliminary thoughts on setting up a new research agenda. *Journal of Contemporary China, 17*(54), 191–204.

Stockmann, D., & Gallagher, M. E. (2018). Remote control: How the media sustain authoritarian rule in China. *Comparative Political Studies, 44*(4), 436–467.

Tang, M., & Huhe, N. (2014). Alternative framing: The effect of the Internet on political support in authoritarian China. *International Political Science Review, 35*(5), 559–576.

Tang, W. (2016). *Populist authoritarianism: Chinese political culture and regime sustainability.* Oxford: Oxford University Press.

Teets, J. C. (2013). Let many civil societies bloom: The rise of consultative authoritarianism in China. *China Quarterly, 213*(213), 19–38.

Tong, J., & Zuo, L. (2014). Weibo communication and government legitimacy in China: A computer-assisted analysis of Weibo messages on two 'mass incidents'. *Information Communication & Society, 17*(1), 66–85.

Tsai, W. (2016). How 'networked authoritarianism' was operationalized in China: Methods and procedures of public opinion control. *Journal of Contemporary China, 25*(101), 731–744.

Tufekci, Z., & Wilson, C. (2012). Social media and the decision to participate in political protest: Observations from Tahrir Square. *Journal of Communication, 62*(2), 363–379.

Wang, J. (2015). Managing social stability: The perspective of a local government in China. *Journal of East Asian Studies, 15*(1), 1–25.

Wang, S. S., & Hong, J. (2010). *Discourse behind the Forbidden Realm: Internet surveillance and its implications on China's blogosphere.* Oxford: Pergamon Press, Inc.

West, D. M. (2010). E-government and the transformation of service delivery and citizen attitudes. *Public Administration Review, 64*(1), 15–27.

White, L. (2005). *Legitimacy: Ambiguities of political success or failure in East and Southeast Asia*: Singapore: World Scientific.

Xu, X., Mao, Z. M., & Halderman, J. A. (2011). *Internet censorship in China: Where does the filtering occur?* Berlin Heidelberg: Springer.

Zeng, J. (2014). The debate on regime legitimacy in China: Bridging the wide gulf between Western and Chinese scholarship. *Journal of Contemporary China, 23*(88), 612–635.

Zheng, Y. (2007). *Technological empowerment: The Internet, state, and society in China.* Redwood: Stanford University Press.

Zheng, Y., & Wu, G. (2005). Information technology, public space, and collective action in China. *Comparative Political Studies, 38*(5), 507–536.

Zuckerman, E. (2013). *Cute cats to the rescue? Participatory media and political expression.* Boston: MIT Press.

5 How (When) Does Technological Innovation Improve Government Efficiency? An Empirical Investigation with Cross-National Evidence

1 Introduction

In "the Eighteenth Brumaire of Louis Bonaparte" in 1852, Karl Max wrote that "Men make their history not of their own accord or under self-chosen conditions, but under given and transmitted conditions".

Modern science and technology innovation change our lifestyles, making life more convenient and work more efficient. It also influences the life cycles of an organization's development. In the case of governments, "technology innovation" is one of the core factors in government reorganization with process reengineering and effectiveness reform.

The extant researches primarily focus on discussing whether government efficiency (relating to government subsidy, government grants) is conducive to technological innovation and diffusion (King et al., 1994; Park, 2014). How does technological innovation in turn influence government efficiency? There is still a lack of rigorous empirical research on the issue. Undoubtfully, numerous other indicators that influence the public department's performance and efficiency cannot be ignored (Hauner & Kyobe, 2010; Rayp & Sijpe, 2007). Due to space limitations, other factors are not the core of this chapter's analysis.

Then, this chapter attempts to fill the gap by studying the panel data collected from 117 countries between 1995 and 2015. The authors confirmed 27 control variables based on innovation diffusion and related literature, then efficiently selected 12 research variables through machine learning. The influence mechanism of technological innovation on government efficiency can be analyzed in different models. The findings reveal that the relationship between technological innovation and government efficiency promotion is not simple linear relation but a more complicated inverted U-shaped relation.

DOI: 10.4324/9781003363712-5

2 Literature on Technological Innovation and Government Efficiency

Government efficiency is not only the focus of researchers but also of citizens. It means that while utilizing limited administrative resources, the executive authority can achieve the goal and optimize the allocation of resources. It was evident that neither government departments nor civil servants can provide effective public services or promote economic and social development without proper administrative capacity. Since the end of the 20th century, countries have improved government efficiency and banishing red tape through various administrative reforms (Lane, 1997; Light, 1998; Moynihan, 2008). Some studies have also noticed that government efficiency is influenced by multiple factors, such as the ability to apply innovative technologies (Welch & Feeney, 2014), civil servants' education level of economic development, and the structure of department, bureaucratic culture, etc.

Technological innovation is closely related to political development and public sector reform. Nowadays, military R&D (which also arouses huge controversy), modern science, and new media technology enable a more recent and closer relationship between the government and citizens than ever before. Technology application and innovation diffusion theory first appeared in the field of social science. It was used to analyze the application and the development of production technology in enterprises and other areas (Goslar, 1987; Oliveira & Martins, 2011). Then an increasing number of government departments realized the benefits of modern technology. New media technology makes the instantaneous transmission of information possible, and the public has more opportunities to learn about the latest political and social information.

Various research perspectives are also developed since the invention of diffusion theory, such as technological determinism and social constructivism. Technological determinism argues that along with the development of science and technology, the improvement of hardware equipment, such as laser printers and supercomputers, will bring unprecedented promotion to organization development. It emphasizes the one-way and decisive influence of technology on an organization (Wyatt, 2008). Namely, once it enters the organizational context, technology is an objective and external force that becomes "technology in-practice" (Orlikowski, 2008). Later on, other scholars focused on the influence of technological innovation on industrial organizations and social organizations and the impact of new information communication technology on politics, such as the application of information technology to research political information communication or political campaigns.

When technological innovation is applied to government agencies, its impact on the government is obvious. For example, the emergence of modern printing technology significantly improved the efficiency of the government to deal with official documents; the video conference system substantially enhanced the efficiency of communication and dissemination of information among departments. Specifically, the impacts of technological innovation on government efficiency are as follows.

First, technological innovation improved the organization's performance (Leavitt, 1965; Perrow, 1967). For instance, Orlikowski, a pre-eminent scholar in this field, pointed out that the interaction between technology and organizations impacts the development and design of organizations' structure (Orlikowski, 2007, 2010).

Second, technological innovation is also conducive to promoting the change of organizations' structure and culture. Henderson and Clark (1990) emphasized that technological innovation remarkably affects organizational innovation as a driving element of organizational change within the company. In addition, Grimpe (2016) also put forward that technological innovation contributes to a company's R&D and will promote the expansion of organization scale. Take Schumpeter's hypothesis as an example; it pointed out that technological innovation will promote business expansion (Kirchhoff & Phillips, 1989).

Third, modern technology reduces the operating costs of organizations. Borghans and Weel (2006) argued that if information technology increases labor productivity, correspondingly, the requirements for workers' skills may also be higher, which can help to improve or enhance the professional level of the organization's human resources. Bresnahan et al. (2002) held the similar view that technological innovation reduces the cost of access to knowledge and information, which improves organizations' competitiveness.

Technological determinism breaks through the limitations of classical organizational management theory and suggests that different technologies adopted by organizations lead to different results (Chandler, 1995). But, such a hypothesis ignores its historical, cultural, and political context all affect the effectiveness of the technological application (Inglehart, 1997). In addition, Cooper and Zmud (1990) tried to analyze the application characteristics of technology in the organization from technical complexity, task complexity, and the degree of matching between the two. It also showed that exogenous technological factors might bring organizations a high degree of uncertainty and complexity during introducing and implementing technologies.

Therefore, scholars began to explore other contextual indicators that influence government efficiency based on social constructivism. Soft constraints like historical culture, social context are crucial to breaking through the bottleneck of government efficiency. Taking the e-government as an example, even though e-government and paperless office system are established with the support of modern technology in various countries, the traditional practice and the professional skills of civil servants are still playing a prominent role in the application of information technology (Moon, 2002; Ndou, 2004). The parts of e-government vary in different countries, and the goals for paperless office have not been achieved in some government departments. So technology-organization-environment (TOE) and technology acceptance model are emphasized by scholars (Baker, 2012; Venkatesh & Davis, 2000).

Researchers, based on the impact of technology-organization interactions on organizational performance, pointed out that technology alone may not necessarily improve the performance of an organization. Some scholars believed in a consistent synergy between technological innovation and organizational innovation (Schmidt & Rammer, 2007). This is also the critical point of modernization theory, i.e., technological development and economic, social, and cultural changes always complement and support each other (Welzel et al., 2003). For example, the industrial revolution promoted the social and political transformation in Western Europe, and in the late 20th century, the post-industrial revolution, information technology, the tide of globalization and democratization, etc., brought about government reforms that met the needs of social development. Therefore, co-evolution or co-production of technology and politics (or society) is commonly used in this field (Bijker et al., 2012; Harbers, 2005).

All in all, from the perspective of technological determinism, technological innovation may have a decisive influence on government performance and will not be interfered with by external factors. From the standpoint of social constructivism, the impact of technological innovation on government efficiency depends on the social, cultural, economic background, and institutional context. In other words, the effect of technological innovation on government efficiency is limited by other external factors (Herring & Roy, 2007; West, 2005). Different researchers held different opinions on the effect of technological innovation in an organization. It is yet to be examined how technological innovation and its application affect government performance.

Based on the analysis above, the authors put forward the following research hypotheses to validate the impact of technological innovation on government efficiency. First of all, the authors propose hypothesis 1 from the perspective of technology determinism.

H1: ceteris paribus, technological innovation has a positive impact on government efficiency.

Second, since Simon Kuznets put forward the concept of "inverted U-curve" in 1955 (Kuznets, 1955), scholars have started exploring whether the inverted U-shaped curve is a hot topic among scholars presented between different variables in social and economic development. However, there is a similar relationship between scientific & technological innovation and government efficiency, which has not received enough attention. Thus hypothesis 2 is proposed:

H2: ceteris paribus, there is an inverted U-shaped relationship between technological innovation and government efficiency.

From the perspective of social constructivism, will other social and cultural factors affect the role of technological innovation in government efficiency? Taking the political system as an example, the authors develop the third hypothesis:

H3: ceteris paribus, the influence of technological innovation on government efficiency varies in different countries with different political systems. Specifically speaking, the higher a country's democratization level is, the more significant the impact of innovation on government efficiency.

3 Research Design for the Effects of Innovation on Government Efficiency

3.1 Independent Variables and Dependent Variables

Innovation and patents are closely linked, so patent data is often used in academic research to measure scientific and technological innovation (Acs et al., 2002; Lanjouw & Schankerman, 2004). This study used the US National Bureau of Economic Research (NBER) patent data as an independent variable, containing detailed information on patents granted by the US Patent and Trademark Office (USPTO) from 1995 to 2015 to develop proxies for innovative national capacity. We preferred USPTO data to those of the World Intellectual Property Office (WIPO) due to a large amount of missing data in the latter and since patents in different countries sometimes represent very different levels of innovation. The patents granted in one country may not be innovative enough in another and may not receive a patent. Since the United States is the largest consumer market of technologies in the world, it has been commonly assumed, in prior studies, that all-important innovations have been patented by the US patent office (Acharya & Subramanian, 2009; Griffith et al., 2006; Hsu et al., 2014). Thus, the number of patents filed at the USPTO, primarily used in peer-reviewed articles (Gao et al., 2017), is equally valid to measure innovative capacity for other countries.

Governance efficiency is a dependent variable used in this chapter, which comes from the Worldwide Governance Indicators and is combined into a single grouping response on the quality of public service provision, the quality of the bureaucracy, the competence of civil servants, the independence of the civil service from political pressures, and the credibility of the government's commitment to policies.[1] Additionally, it is generally distributed with a mean of 0 and a standard deviation of 1 in each year's measurement. This implies that virtually all scores of governance efficiency lie between –2.5 and 2.5, with higher scores representing better effectiveness (Kaufmann et al., 2011).

3.2 Machine Learning and Control Variable Screening

The analyses of social, political, and economic theories from previous literature help get some main variables related to government efficiency. According to the author's preliminary estimates, in existing researches, the number of frequently used control variables that influence government efficiency is as high as 27, and it remains a tough job to choose variables that best fit the model. The random forest or random decision forest, which is the most famous method in machine learning, can help effectively select a more relevant group of control variables. The technique can also reduce the impact of noise variables and selective bias.

Random forest, put forward by Breiman Leo and Adele Cutler of the University of California at Berkeley in 2001, is a compelling feature selection method in the machine-learning family (Cutler & Zhao, 2001). It can be used for classification, regression, survival analysis, feature selection, and other tasks that operate by constructing a multitude of decision trees during training and producing the class that is the mode of the classes (classification) or mean prediction (regression) of the individual trees (Genuer et al., 2010).

Using the values of Gini-importance and permutation importance, the random forest can better predict the importance degree of different variables in analyzing an unbalanced set of panel data. We created the sequence of variables, according to their Gini-importance values, in the random forest model containing all controlled variables and dependent ones. These controlled variables, preliminarily selected from 27 relevant ones, are shown in Table A5.1 in Appendix.

In this chapter, we controlled the following kinds of potential determinants of government efficiency. First, GDP per capita is a visible variable referring to the degree of prosperity of a country. Furthermore, the authors also considered setting the sum of exports and imports of goods and services (% of GDP) as another controlled one. All the data here came from the World Bank. In addition, this chapter also uses the economic freedom index from the Heritage Foundation and Wall Street Journal to measure the vibrant level of one country. From the political dimension, we take variables like political stability (World Governance Indicator), political corruption (Transparency International), democracy (Freedom House/Imputed Polity), and political imprisonment (Human Rights Watch) into consideration. This chapter uses tax burden data from the World Bank and data involving log of population density, cultural diversity, telephone lines (per 100 people), and secure Internet servers (per 1 million people). Variables above are chosen according to the analysis result of machine learning and extant literature.

In conclusion, we select variables in three steps: (1) make use of machine learning method and random forest of original data to determine the importance of different variables to the model; (2) discover a linear relationship between two explanatory variables through collinearity diagnosis; and (3) conduct logical analysis on the selected variables based on existing literature and further confirm the controlled variables. In general, the choice is of more feasibility and trustworthiness for further analysis.

3.3 Unbalance Assessment of Data

Based on our analysis above and the results from the random forest, we chose this collection of variables from 1995 to 2015 as the panel data. Although the USPTO dataset contains data from 224 countries, large portions of data (10% or more for any year) of some countries are missing. To ensure the quality of the data, these countries were first omitted in our study, so the panel data consists of variables of 156 countries from 1995 to 2015. Then the authors analyzed and evaluated the quality of these variables mainly by examining the data missing percentage (see Table 5.1 for details).

The authors took the third quartile (0.1802) missing data as a critical parameter to further exclude some countries (for which the degree of missing data is higher than the critical parameter). Figure 5.1 describes the proportion of missing data among different countries. It shows that the missing data of some countries is around or even more than 10%. Therefore, the authors then excluded these countries and finally collected the panel data of 117 countries between 1995 and 2015.

The descriptive statistics of all the variables are in Table 5.2. It can be seen that the number of observations (or data points) is very different among variables. The means of different variables calculated in this study are consistent with the World Bank, suggesting that our selected sample of countries is highly representative.

Figure 5.2 describes the relationship between technological innovation and governance efficiency by the scatter plot and the polynomial

Table 5.1 Descriptive statistics for the status of missing data from the country and year

Variable	*Obs*	*Mean*	*3rd*	*Std. Dev.*	*Min*	*Max*
Country	156	0.1342	0.1802	0.1066	0.0490	0.5552
Year	20	0.1333	0.1749	0.0678	0.0626	0.2834

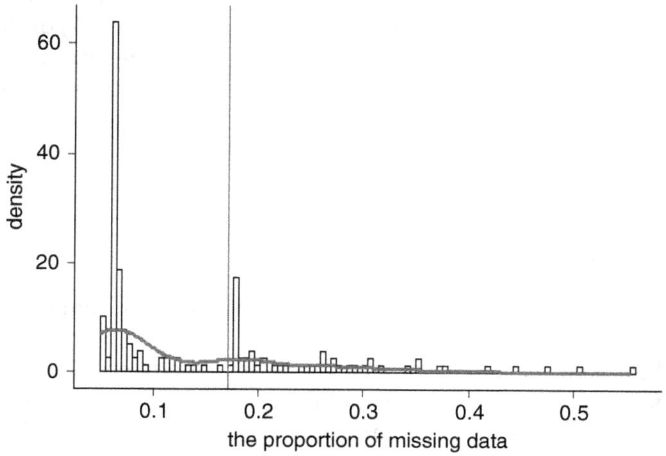

Figure 5.1 The proportion of missing data

Table 5.2 Descriptive statistics for primary selected variables

Variable	*Definition*	*Obs*	*Mean*	*Std. Dev.*	*Min*	*Max*
wbgi_gee	Governance Efficiency	1844	0.1299	0.9637	–2.0309	2.4297
lpat_uspt	The log of patent grants	2283	2.5096	2.7995	0	12.2663
wdi_trade	The sum of exports and imports of goods and services (% of GDP)	2255	81.3096	43.1492	15.5803	439.6567
lgdppc	Log of GDP per capita, PPP (constant 2005 international $)	2281	8.6376	1.4339	5.8826	11.4251
lpop_dnst	Log of Population density (people per sq. km of land area)	2278	4.1212	1.3881	0.3915	8.9537
wbgi_pse	Political Stability	1844	–0.073	0.8895	–2.3901	1.6681
fh_ipolity2	Level of Democracy (Freedom House/Imputed Polity)	2283	6.7351	3.0721	0	10
hf_efi score	Economic Freedom Index	2244	61.0316	10.4682	21.4000	89.40
vdem_corr	Political corruption	1945	0.4918	0.2909	0.0098	0.9434
fe_cultdiv	Cultural Diversity	2225	0.2875	0.2028	0	0.7328
wdi_telephone	Telephone lines (per 100 people)	2276	20.7409	18.6014	0	74.7625
ciri_polpris	Political Imprisonment	1916	1.2171	0.8238	0	2
Tax burden	Tax burden	1951	72.4530	14.9415	29.8	99.9
wdi_internetserv	Secure Internet servers (per 1 million people)	1444	184.0495	438.4676	0.0072	3214.394

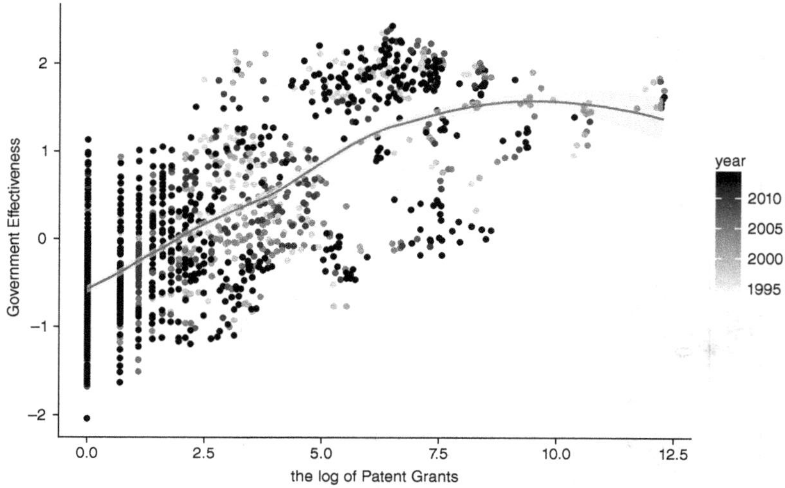

Figure 5.2 The relationship between governance efficiency and the country's innovation

simulating curve. Besides, it also shows that, in general, a positive correlation, sometimes an inverted-U curve, can be seen between technological innovation and government efficiency. The following part will further analyze the impact mechanism between these two variables based on the fixed-effects model.

3.3 Model Construction

To further examine our earlier stated hypotheses and explore the relationship between technological innovation and governance efficiency, the authors established the following different regression models.

3.3.1 Multiple Linear Regression Model

Regression analysis, an essential branch of modern applied statistics, is a traditional scientific method that has already been widely used in all fields of science, including social science studies. It is of great potential to dig out the most valuable information from a large original dataset, capturing the main features of the dataset. In addition, it is conducive to finding and validating the correlation relationship between different variables in a multiple linear regression model through statistical tests.

First, the multiple linear regression model will be used to explore this relationship between variables. We can extract as much information about different variables as possible by this model. Meanwhile, the magnitude of those coefficients through this model can reflect the changing trends of the research subject from 1995 to 2015. Based on that, the authors established the following mathematical model,

$$y = \beta_0 + \beta_1 x_1 + \beta_2 x_2 + ...\beta_p x_p + \varepsilon \tag{1}$$
$$\varepsilon - N(0,\sigma^2)$$

where β_0, β_0 … β_0 are the regression coefficients, N denotes the number of samples, and ε represents residuals that follow a normal distribution. This chapter will use the Maximum Likelihood Estimator (MLE) to estimate these regression coefficients.

When considering the time (year) trend and heteroscedasticity, the estimated method of Feasible Generalized Least Squared (FGLS) is the best choice in this study. Comparing other regressing results, FGLS has a better solution than the general OLS estimated method in dealing with the time trend and heteroscedasticity.

3.3.2 Fixed Effects Model

The data used in this chapter start as unbalanced panel data. The extraction of balanced panel data will unavoidably reduce the sample size as well as the efficiency of estimation, and subjective deletion of observations will inevitably affect the randomness of the data sample. To achieve our research objectives, fixed effects panel data models controlled for years and country effects were employed, the influence of omitted variables due to those fixed effects was limited, and heteroscedasticity problems in these tests were mitigated. These fixed effects models controlled unobserved variables that differed across regions but did not vary across time, also differed across time but did not vary across states. Then, the authors established the following fixed effects model:

$$y = \beta_0 + x_{it}\beta_1 + z_{it}\beta_2 + \alpha_i + \xi_t + \varepsilon_{it} \tag{2}$$

where i denotes any of the countries in our sample, and i=1, …, 117; t denotes the year, and t=1, …, 20; y_{it} represents the explained variable; x_{it} is a vector of time-variant explanatory variable; z_{it} is the matrix of control variables; β denotes the coefficients to be estimated; α_i is the fixed country effects, which is potentially correlated with x_{it}; ξ_t is the fixed time (year) effects; ε_{it} denotes the error term. Strong assumptions are set to formula (1):

$$E(\varepsilon_{it}\ \alpha_{it}, x_{it}) = 0, i = 1, 2, ...N$$

In statistics, there are many estimated methods to calculate the coefficients of the variables. We used the estimated Least Square Dummy Variables (LSDV) method to regress the primary model when considering the fixed country effect. In this chapter, the authors compared the results of different kinds of regressing estimated methods with diverse fixed effects (time, country, or both).

4 Empirical Results of Different Models

To overcome the intense correlation among the variables and ensure that the correlation coefficient estimated in the model is free of distortion or inaccuracy, the authors first performed a multi-collinearity test. Table 5.3 indicates that the VIF (Variance Inflation Factor) values of all the variables were less than 10, suggesting that multicollinearity does not exist among variables. Thus, all the variables can be used in the following analysis in the multiple linear regression model.

Table 5.3 Multi-collinearity test

Variable	*VIF*	*SQRT VIF*	*Tolerance*	*R-Squared*
The log of patent grants	4.08	2.02	0.2453	0.7547
The sum of exports and imports of goods and services (% of GDP)	1.33	1.15	0.7526	0.2474
Log of GDP per capita, PPP (constant 2005 international $)	6.77	2.60	0.1476	0.8524
Log of Population density (people per sq. km of land area)	1.44	1.20	0.6963	0.3037
Political Stability	2.88	1.70	0.3467	0.6533
Level of Democracy (Freedom House/Imputed Polity)	3.05	1.75	0.3282	0.6718
Economic Freedom Index	3.04	1.74	0.3288	0.6712
Political corruption	3.86	1.96	0.2592	0.7408
Cultural Diversity	1.23	1.11	0.8107	0.1893
Telephone lines (per 100 people)	5.49	2.34	0.1823	0.8177
Tax burden	1.87	1.37	0.5353	0.4647
Political Imprisonment	2.28	1.51	0.4389	0.5611
Secure Internet servers (per 1 million people)	1.91	1.38	0.5243	0.4757
Mean VIF	3.02			

4.1 Results of Multiple Linear Regression

In Table 5.4, the authors compared the regression result of adding the variable of the square log of patent grants or not in models 1 and 2, respectively. Model 3 shows FGLS regression results. Based on the reference system of countries in East Asia and the Pacific region, model 4 describes the average impact of technological innovation on the efficiency of governments in the different areas.

Regression results of different models in Table 5.4 show that technological innovation has a significantly positive effect on government efficiency. This finding initially supports the idea of technology determinism. Thus, hypothesis 1 is confirmed. Meanwhile, results of other variables also show that the economic growth level of a country, population density, political stability, democratization, financial freedom, and cultural diversity are positively correlated with public sector performance, which is in line with the current research results (Perry & Christensen, 2015; Pierre, 2003; Wholey, 2007). At the same time, political corruption, government imprisonment, and the tax burden will negatively impact government efficiency, which is also consistent with both reality and the extant research results (Burman & Phaup, 2012; Helland & Sørensen, 2015; Rose-Ackerman & Palifka, 2016).

Model 2 in Table 5.4 shows that the square log of patent grants has a significantly negative correlation with government efficiency, which means the influence imposed by technological innovation on government efficiency presents an inverted U-shaped feature. It shows that as a country's diffusion of technological innovation gradually improves, the impact of technology on government efficiency increases at first and then reduces with time. In other words, technological innovation has a marginal diminishing effect on the improvement of government efficiency. Thus, hypothesis 2 is tested. This shows that there is no simple linear relationship between technological innovation and government efficiency, as in the traditional view.

Technological determinism is challenged. The analysis of social constructivism above also points out that geographical, cultural, and historical factors of different countries also affect how the performance of public sectors can be promoted. As for different regions, technological innovation positively impacts government efficiency in the Middle East, North Africa, and South Asia. It has no positive impact on other countries and even hurts the government efficiency of Latin America and Caribbean countries. Therefore, further exploration of this phenomenon is needed.

Table 5.4 Results of multiple linear regression

	Model 1	*Model 2*	*Model 3*	*Model 4*
Variables	Mult-reg	Mult-reg	FGLS	Mult-reg
The log of patent grants	0.0451***	0.0984***	0.0391***	0.0337***
	(0.01)	(0.01)	(0.00)	(0.01)
The square log of patent grants		−0.0064***		
		(0.00)		
The sum of exports and imports of goods and services (% of GDP)	0.0001	−0.0001	0.0003	−0.0005
	(0.00)	(0.00)	(0.00)	(0.00)
Log of GDP per capita, PPP (constant 2005 international $)	0.1014***	0.0793***	0.0858***	0.1023***
	(0.02)	(0.02)	(0.01)	(0.02)
Log of Population density (people per sq. km of land area)	0.0499***	0.0537***	0.0512***	0.0416***
	(0.01)	(0.01)	(0.01)	(0.01)
Political Stability	0.1376***	0.1458***	0.1064***	0.1410***
	(0.02)	(0.02)	(0.01)	(0.02)
Level of Democracy (Freedom House/Imputed Polity)	0.0373***	0.0296***	0.0258***	0.0482***
	(0.01)	(0.01)	(0.00)	(0.01)
Economic Freedom Index	0.0300***	0.0308***	0.0284***	0.0302***
	(0.00)	(0.00)	(0.00)	(0.00)
Political corruption	−0.6941***	−0.6795***	−0.8347***	−0.6926***
	(0.07)	(0.06)	(0.04)	(0.06)
Cultural Diversity	0.1537**	0.1461**	0.2329***	0.1130*
	(0.05)	(0.05)	(0.03)	(0.05)
Telephone lines (per 100 people)	0.0033*	0.0039**	0.0051***	0.0016
	(0.00)	(0.00)	(0.00)	(0.00)
Tax burden	−0.0124***	−0.0126***	−0.0115***	−0.0126***
	(0.00)	(0.00)	(0.00)	(0.00)

	Model 1	*Model 2*	*Model 3*	*Model 4*
Political Imprisonment	−0.1486***	−0.1344***	−0.1104***	−0.1161***
	(0.02)	(0.02)	(0.01)	(0.02)
Secure Internet servers (per 1 million people)	0.0001**	0.0001**	0.0001***	0.0001**
	(0.00)	(0.00)	(0.00)	(0.00)
East Asia & Pacific				0.0000
				(–)
Europe & Central Asia				0.0098
				(0.04)
Latin America & Caribbean				−0.1706***
				(0.04)
Middle East & North Africa				0.1670***
				(0.05)
South Asia				0.1321*
				(0.06)
Sub-Saharan Africa				−0.0708
				(0.04)
Constant	−1.8934***	−1.7632***	−1.6027***	−1.8317***
	(0.18)	(0.18)	(0.13)	(0.18)
Observation	792	792	792	792
Num. country	117	117	117	117
Time trends	No	No	Yes	No
Adj-R^2	0.925	0.927	–	0.932

Note: Standard errors are in parentheses; *, ** and *** denotes significance levels of 5%, 1% and 0.1%, respectively.

4.2 Results of Fixed Effect Model

This part, based on the fixed effects model, examines the impact of technological innovation on governance efficiency more precisely.

Models 1 and 2 in Table 5.5 show that regarding the fixed effect model or the random effect model result, the innovation has a prominent impact on government efficiency. However, according to the Hausman test, the authors adopted the fixed effect model. It can be seen from model 3 in Table 5.5 that technological innovation has not only contemporary positive effects but also remarkable lingering effects on government efficiency.

This is mainly due to two factors. On the one hand, compared with the quick adoption of the latest technologies by enterprises, new technologies in government are relatively backward. On the other hand, the diffusion of technological innovation among different countries varies. It is difficult for some governments to obtain the convenience of scientific and technological innovations.

Comparing models 1 and 4 in Table 5.5, the result shows that whether the time effect is controlled or not, the impact of technological innovation on government efficiency is relatively stable, and that of other control variables on government efficiency is also consistent with the results in Table 5.4, all of which further demonstrate that the findings of this chapter have high validity and reliability.

4.3 Comparing the Effects of Innovation between High and Low Levels of Democracy

From the perspective of social constructivism analysis, the difference of technological innovation in different political systems is often apparent since different countries have different regimes and historical and cultural backgrounds. Besides, previous studies have shown that the same technological innovation has different application effects in countries with different political systems. Concerning Internet technology, for example, it may become a tool for assisting governments in further monitoring and censoring citizens' expression in authoritarian countries (Chadwick & Howard, 2010) or serve as an effective bridge of communication between governments and citizens in democratic countries.

Figure 5.3 shows the distribution of each country democratic is observed that, in 117 countries, democracy is characterized by bimodal distribution. According to the median of democracy (7.833333) in 117 countries from 1995 to 2014, the authors divided the sample nations

Table 5.5 Results of fixed effect model

	Model 1	*Model 2*	*Model 3*	*Model 4*
Variables	FE	RE	FE	FE
The log of patent grants	0.0202*	0.0499***		0.0196*
	(0.01)	(0.01)		(0.01)
The lag of log of patent grants			0.0215*	
			(0.01)	
The sum of exports and imports of goods and	–0.0011**	–0.0017***	–0.0012***	–0.0006
services (% of GDP)	(0.00)	(0.00)	(0.00)	(0.00)
Log of GDP per capita, PPP (constant 2005	0.2469***	0.1643***	0.2432***	0.3577***
international $)	(0.03)	(0.02)	(0.03)	(0.04)
Log of Population density (people per sq. km of	–0.6904***	–0.0136	–0.7262***	–0.4960***
land area)	(0.06)	(0.02)	(0.06)	(0.08)
Political Stability	0.1481***	0.1924***	0.1505***	0.1429***
	(0.01)	(0.01)	(0.01)	(0.01)
Level of Democracy (Freedom House/Imputed	0.0063	0.0055	0.0063	0.0054
Polity)	(0.01)	(0.01)	(0.01)	(0.01)
Economic Freedom Index	0.0036**	0.0071***	0.0041***	0.0031**
	(0.00)	(0.00)	(0.00)	(0.00)
Political corruption	–0.4325***	–0.8759***	–0.4276***	–0.4663***
	(0.09)	(0.08)	(0.08)	(0.09)
Constant	0.8097**	–1.2623***	0.9678***	–0.8845
	(0.26)	(0.20)	(0.27)	(0.49)
Observation	1510	1510	1491	1510
Num. of country	117	117	117	117
Country-effect	Yes	Yes	Yes	Yes
Year-effect	No	No	No	Yes
Hausman test based on Model 2	21942***	–	2958***	18754***
Adj-R^2	0.195	–	0.206	0.213

Note: standard errors are in parentheses; *, ** and *** denotes significance levels of 5%, 1% and 0.1%, respectively.

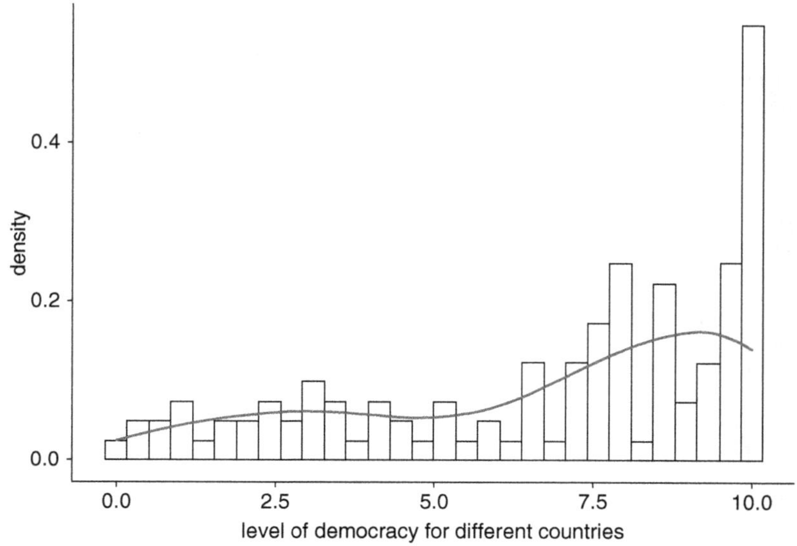

Figure 5.3 Distribution of democracy scores

in this chapter into developed democracy group and developed democracy group. Furthermore, it is investigated in this chapter whether technological innovation in countries with different democratic systems will generate varied effects or not.

Table 5.6 shows the results of regression analysis of developed democratic countries and less-developed democracies, respectively. Although technological innovation does have positive effects on government efficiency in different sample groups, there are remarkable differences in the coefficient among countries with different levels of democracy. For instance, the impact of technological innovation on government efficiency in less-developed democratic countries is only a third of that in developed ones. This finding suggests that the democratization system can indirectly affect public sector performance through technological innovation. Thus, hypothesis 3 can be tested. Meanwhile, the authors also found that the impact brought by variables such as political stability, political freedom, and political corruption in less-developed democratic countries is remarkably higher than that in developed ones. In other words, less-developed democratic countries are more sensitive to this kind of variable.

Table 5.6 The result of regression analysis of countries with various democracy level

Level of democracy	*High*	*Low*	*All*
Variables	Model 1	Model 2	Model 3
The log of patent grants	0.0587***	−0.0127	−0.0012
	(0.01)	(0.01)	(0.01)
Interaction of the log of patent grant and Democracy			0.0479**
			(0.02)
The sum of exports and imports of goods and services (% of GDP)	−0.0015***	−0.0004	−0.0006
	(0.00)	(0.00)	(0.00)
Log of GDP per capita, PPP (constant 2005 international $)	0.2438***	0.2522***	0.3579***
	(0.04)	(0.04)	(0.04)
Log of Population density (people per sq. km of land area)	−0.9142***	−0.5133***	−0.4822***
	(0.10)	(0.08)	(0.08)
Political Stability	0.1529***	0.1440***	0.1457***
	(0.02)	(0.02)	(0.01)
Economic Freedom Index	0.0015	0.0060***	0.0034**
	(0.00)	(0.00)	(0.00)
Political corruption	−0.6911***	0.0790	−0.4874***
	(0.11)	(0.14)	(0.08)
Constant	2.0065***	−0.2930	−0.9008
	(0.42)	(0.33)	(0.49)
Observations	710	800	1510
Num. of country	59	58	117
Country-effect	Yes	Yes	Yes
Year-effect	No	No	Yes
Adj-R^2	0.280	0.133	0.217

Note: Standard errors are in parentheses; *, ** and *** denotes significance levels of 5%, 1% and 0.1%, respectively.

5 Robust Test

To further validate the stability and reliability of the results above, the authors made a robust test to the fixed-effect model, which is mainly carried out in two parts. First, the authors added more controlled variables to see whether they brought significant changes to the result. Second, considering the influence of data integrity and data balance, the authors compared the differences of regression analysis on initial data and selected data. This chapter involves unadjusted data in the regression analysis part. The results of models 2 and 3 in Table 5.7

Table 5.7 Results of robust test

	Model 1	*Model 2*	*Model 3*
Variables	Final data	Final data	Original data
The log of patent grants	0.0196*	0.0226*	0.0277**
	(0.01)	(0.01)	(0.01)
The sum of exports and imports of goods and services (% of GDP)	–0.0006	–0.0007	–0.0006
	(0.00)	(0.00)	(0.00)
Log of GDP per capita, PPP (constant 2005 international $)	0.3577***	0.3524***	0.3567***
	(0.04)	(0.04)	(0.04)
Log of GDP per capita, PPP (constant 2005 international $)	–0.4960***	–0.5031***	–0.1573*
	(0.08)	(0.09)	(0.06)
Political Stability	0.1429***	0.1411***	0.1518***
	(0.01)	(0.02)	(0.01)
Level of Democracy (Freedom House/Imputed Polity)	0.0054	0.0077	0.0013
	(0.01)	(0.01)	(0.01)
Economic Freedom Index	0.0031**	0.0024	0.0049***
	(0.00)	(0.00)	(0.00)
Political corruption	–0.4663***	–0.4748***	–0.4778***
	(0.09)	(0.09)	(0.08)
Telephone lines (per 100 people)		–0.0011	
		(0.00)	
Political Imprisonment		–0.0015	
		(0.01)	
Constant	–0.8845	–0.7687	–2.3252***
	(0.49)	(0.55)	(0.43)
Observations	1510	1391	1681
Num. of country	117	117	131
Country-effect	Yes	Yes	Yes
Year-effect	Yes	Yes	Yes
Adj-R^2	0.213	0.195	0.178

Note: Standard errors are in parentheses; *, ** and *** denotes significance levels of 5%, 1% and 0.1%, respectively.

show that technological innovation still has a remarkable impact on government efficiency, which is consistent with previous results.

6 Conclusion

The authors discussed the impacts of technological innovation on government efficiency based on the data, such as US National

Bureau of Economic Research (NBER) patent data, the World Bank social-economic data, and Transparency International data. The authors' analysis results are demonstrated as follows.

First, technological innovation does prominently simulate the upgrade of government efficiency. And along with the rapid improvement of science and technology, government efficiency improves synchronously at the first stage.

Second, the improvement of government efficiency, which is closely linked to technological innovation, is not simply presented in a linear relationship. Instead, the constantly changing trend generally shows an inverted U-shaped trajectory.

Finally, the impacts of technological innovation on government efficiency vary significantly in different contexts of political systems. For instance, technological innovation could play a preferable role in democratic states, in which government efficiency gains significant promotion. Whereas in less-developed democratic countries, technological innovation could not give full play to its advantages so that the improvement of government efficiency is reflected in a significantly lower degree, corresponding to the phenomenon that despite in some authoritarian states where e-government system is broadly applied, the public still hasn't enjoyed its conveniences of open and transparent official information. It's worth saying that the positive effects brought by technological advancement to the current government involve relevant political systems.

The theoretical implications concluded from this chapter is that, even though technological determinism and social constructivism manifest the explanatory values and significance to a certain extent, we should not be too obsessed with such analytical approaches. Since complicated and dynamic factors can influence government efficiency, the traditional analytical path based on a single technological determinism or social constructivism is insufficient to map the impact mechanism. On the one hand, technological innovation has a ceiling effect in promoting government efficiency. Therefore, when the improvement of government efficiency hits the bottleneck, other indirect factors need to be examined. On the other hand, certain variables related to social constructivism, like the political system and cultural background, have unstable government efficiency. Despite the approval of several scholars supporting social constructivism, more rigorous verification should be carried out.

All the controlled variables cited in this chapter were based on different contexts of economy, politics, and society, which fundamentally increase the explanatory power of the model and the integrity of the control variables. However, due to the limitation of missing data, some theoretically significant variables, such as e-government and administrative management expenditures, fail to be included in this model. In-depth future studies could focus on the following aspects. The first is to outline the diverse impacts of technological innovation on government efficiency in various regions (i.e., different levels of economic development). The second one is to deeply explore the development law of government efficiency globally in a given time cycle. The third is to focus on the core factors that restrict or promote government efficiency. In addition, the impact of different types of innovation should be further explored. Although this chapter did not distinguish the differences between innovation types, with constant upgrades in data quality, this problem can and should be investigated in the future.

References

Acharya, V. V., & Subramanian, K. V. (2009). Bankruptcy codes and innovation. *Review of Financial Studies, 22*(12), 4949–4988.

Acs, Z. J., Anselin, L., & Varga, A. (2002). Patents and innovation count as measures of regional production of new knowledge. *Research Policy, 31*(7), 1069–1085.

Baker, J. (2012). The technology–organization–environment framework. In Y. K. Dwivedi, M. R. Wade, & S. L. Schneberger (Eds.), *Information systems theory* (pp. 231–245). Springer.

Bijker, W. E., Hughes, T. P., Pinch, T., & Douglas, D. G. (2012). *The social construction of technological systems: New directions in the sociology and history of technology*. MIT Press.

Borghans, L., & Weel, B. (2006). The division of labour, worker organisation, and technological change. *The Economic Journal, 116*(509), F45–F72.

Bresnahan, T. F., Brynjolfsson, E., & Hitt, L. M. (2002). Information technology, workplace organization, and the demand for skilled labor: Firm-level evidence. *The Quarterly Journal of Economics, 117*(1), 339–376.

Burman, L. E., & Phaup, M. (2012). Tax expenditures, the size and efficiency of government, and implications for budget reform. *Tax Policy & the Economy, 26*(1), 93–124.

Chadwick, A., & Howard, P. N. (2010). *Routledge handbook of Internet politics*. Taylor & Francis.

Chandler, D. (1995). Technological or media determinism. Online] Available at: http://www.aber.ac.uk/media. Documents/tecdet/tecdet.html.

Cooper, R. B., & Zmud, R. W. (1990). Information technology implementation research: A technological diffusion approach. *Management Science, 36*(2), 123–139.

Cutler, A., & Zhao, G. (2001). Pert-perfect random tree ensembles. *Computing Science and Statistics, 33*, 490–497.

Gao, Y., Zang, L., Roth, A., & Wang, P. (2017). Does democracy cause innovation? An empirical test of the popper hypothesis. *Research Policy, 46*(7), 1272–1283.

Genuer, R., Poggi, J.-M., & Tuleau-Malot, C. (2010). Variable selection using random forests. *Pattern Recognition Letters, 31*(14), 2225–2236.

Goslar, M. D. (1987). Marketing and the adoption of microcomputers: An application of diffusion theory. *Journal of the Academy of Marketing Science, 15*(2), 42–48.

Griffith, R., Harrison, R., & Van Reenen, J. (2006). How special is the special relationship? Using the impact of US R&D spillovers on UK firms as a test of technology sourcing. *The American Economic Review, 96*(5), 1859–1875.

Grimpe, C. (2016). Making use of the unused: shelf warmer technologies in research and development. *Technovation, 26*(7), 770–774.

Harbers, H. (2005). *Inside the politics of technology: Agency and normativity in the co-production of technology and society*. Amsterdam University Press.

Hauner, D., & Kyobe, A. (2010). Determinants of government efficiency. *World Development, 38*(11), 1527–1542.

Helland, L., & Sørensen, R. J. (2015). Partisan bias, electoral volatility, and government efficiency. *Electoral Studies, 39*, 117–128.

Henderson, R. M., & Clark, K. B. (1990). Architectural innovation: The reconfiguration of existing product technologies and the failure of established firms. *Administrative Science Quarterly, 35*(1), 9–30.

Herring, H., & Roy, R. (2007). Technological innovation, energy efficient design and the rebound effect. *Technovation, 27*(4), 194–203.

Hsu, P.-H., Tian, X., & Xu, Y. (2014). Financial development and innovation: Cross-country evidence. *Journal of Financial Economics, 112*(1), 116–135.

Inglehart, R. (1997). *Modernization and postmodernization: Cultural, economic, and political change in 43 societies*. Princeton: Princeton University Press.

Kaufmann, D., Kraay, A., & Mastruzzi, M. (2011). The worldwide governance indicators: Methodology and analytical issues. *Social Science Electronic Publishing, 3*(2), 220–246.

King, J. L., Gurbaxani, V., Kraemer, K. L., McFarlan, F. W., Raman, K., & Yap, C.-S. (1994). Institutional factors in information technology innovation. *Information Systems Research, 5*(2), 139–169.

Kirchhoff, B. A., & Phillips, B. D. (1989). Innovation and growth among new firms in the US economy. *Frontiers of Entrepreneurship Research, 9*, 173–188.

Kuznets, S. (1955). Economic growth and income inequality. *American Economic Review, 45*(1), 1–28.

Lane, J.-E. (1997). *Public sector reform: Rationale, trends and problems*. Sage.

Lanjouw, J. O., & Schankerman, M. (2004). Patent quality and research productivity: Measuring innovation with multiple indicators. *The Economic Journal, 114*(495), 441–465.

Leavitt, H. J. (1965). Applied organizational change in industry, structural, technological and humanistic approaches. In J. G. March (Ed.), *Handbook of organizations* (p. 264). London: Routledge.

Light, P. C. (1998). *The tides of reform: Making government work, 1945–1995.* New Haven: Yale University Press.

Moon, M. J. (2002). The evolution of e-government among municipalities: Rhetoric or reality? *Public Administration Review, 62*(4), 424–433.

Moynihan, D. P. (2008). *The dynamics of performance management: Constructing information and reform.* Georgetown University Press.

Ndou, V. D. (2004). e-Government for developing countries: Opportunities and challenges. *The Electronic Journal of Information Systems in Developing Countries, 18*(1), 1–24.

Oliveira, T., & Martins, M. F. (2011). Literature review of information technology adoption models at firm Level. *The Electronic Journal Information Systems Evaluation, 14*(1), 110–121.

Orlikowski, W. J. (2007). Sociomaterial practice: Exploring technology at work. *Organization Studies, 28*(9), 1435–1448.

Orlikowski, W. J. (2008). Using technology and constituting structures: A practice lens for studying technology in organizations. In M. S. Ackerman, C. A. Halverson, T. Erickson, & W. A. Kellogg, (Eds.), *Resources, Co-evolution and Artifacts* (pp. 255–305). New York: Springer.

Orlikowski, W. J. (2010). The sociomateriality of organisational life: Considering technology in management research. *Cambridge Journal of economics, 34*(1), 125–141.

Park, S. (2014). Evaluating the efficiency and productivity change within government subsidy recipients of a national technology innovation research and development program. *R & D Management, 45*(5), 549–568.

Perrow, C. (1967). A framework for the comparative analysis of organization. *American Sociological Review, 32*(2), 194–208.

Perry, J. L., & Christensen, R. K. (2015). *Handbook of public administration.* New Jersey: John Wiley & Sons.

Pierre, B. G. P. J. (2003). *Handbook of public administration.* Sage.

Rayp, G., & Sijpe, N. V. D. (2007). Measuring and explaining government efficiency in developing countries. *Journal of Development Studies, 43*(2), 360–381.

Rose-Ackerman, S., & Palifka, B. J. (2016). *Corruption and government: Causes, consequences, and reform*: Cambridge University Press.

Schmidt, T., & Rammer, C. (2007). *Non-technological and technological innovation: Strange bedfellows?* ZEW - Centre for European Economic Research Discussion Paper No. 07-052.

Venkatesh, V., & Davis, F. D. (2000). A theoretical extension of the technology acceptance model: Four longitudinal field studies. *Management Science, 46*(2), 186–204.

Welch, E. W., & Feeney, M. K. (2014). Technology in government: How organizational culture mediates information and communication technology outcomes. *Government Information Quarterly, 31*(4), 506–512.

Welzel, C., Inglehart, R., & Kligemann, H. D. (2003). The theory of human development: A cross-cultural analysis. *European Journal of Political Research, 42*(3), 341–379.

West, D. M. (2005). *Digital government: Technology and public sector performance.* Princeton University Press.

Wholey, J. S. (2007). *Monitoring performance in the public sector: Future directions from international experience.* Transaction Publishers.

Wyatt, S. (2008). Technological determinism is dead: Long live technological determinism. In E. J. Hackett, M. Lynch, & J. Wajcman (Eds.), *The handbook of science and technology studies* (Vol. 3, pp. 165–180). Cambridge, MA: MIT Press.

Appendix 1

Table A5.1 The importance degree of variables from random forest

Variables	*Gini(%)*	*Rank*	*Variables*	*Gini(%)*	*Rank*
Log of GDP per capita, PPP (constant 2005 international $)	24.655	1	Language Fractionalization	14.324	15
Political corruption	22.203	2	Freedom of the Press, Score	14.301	16
patent grants	19.771	3	Regime Durability	13.326	17
Urban population (% of total)	18.576	4	Government expenditure on education as % of GDP (%)	12.498	18
R&D per capita in PPP 2005 constant international $	18.224	5	Cultural Diversity	12.472	19
The sum of exports and imports of goods and services (% of GDP)	17.403	6	Rule of Law	12.251	20
Tax burden	17.147	7	Level of Democracy (Freedom House/ Imputed Polity)	11.327	21
Log of Population density (people per sq. km of land area)	17.011	8	Economic Freedom Index	10.965	22
Political Stability	15.655	9	Internet users (per 100 people)	8.531	23

Variables	*Gini(%)*	*Rank*	*Variables*	*Gini(%)*	*Rank*
Secure Internet servers (per 1 million people)	15.501	10	Financial Freedom	8.364	24
Money Freedom	14.962	11	Telephone lines (per 100 people)	8.164	25
Ethnic Fractionalization	14.954	12	Press Freedom Index	8.113	26
Economic World Institutional Quality Ranking	14.465	13	Political Imprisonment	7.678	27
Labor Freedom	14.402	14			

Table A5.2 Collinear relationship of the variables

Variables	*VIF*	*SQRT VIF*	*Tolerance*	*R-Squared*
patent grants	2.57	1.6	0.3888	0.6112
The sum of exports and imports of goods and services (% of GDP)	2.14	1.46	0.4672	0.5328
Log of Population density (people per sq. km of land area)	2.17	1.47	0.4599	0.5401
Political Stability	6.68	2.58	0.1497	0.8503
Level of Democracy (Freedom House/Imputed Polity)	10.04	3.17	0.0996	0.9004
Economic Freedom Index	12.1	3.48	0.0827	0.9173
Log of GDP per capita, PPP (constant 2005 international $)	22.15	4.71	0.0452	0.9548
Political corruption	15.73	3.97	0.0636	0.9364
Cultural Diversity	5.06	2.25	0.1978	0.8022
Telephone lines (per 100 people)	5.88	2.43	0.17	0.83
Political Imprisonment	2.86	1.69	0.3502	0.6498
Tax burden	3.94	1.98	0.2539	0.7461
Secure Internet servers (per 1 million people)	4.26	2.06	0.2348	0.7652
Regime Durability	3.48	1.87	0.287	0.713

(*Continued*)

Variables	*VIF*	*SQRT VIF*	*Tolerance*	*R-Squared*
Economic World Institutional Quality Ranking	22.22	4.71	0.045	0.955
Log of R&D per capita in PPP 2005 constant international $	17.67	4.2	0.0566	0.9434
Urban population (% of total)	3.61	1.9	0.2768	0.7232
Labor Freedom	2.16	1.47	0.4637	0.5363
Financial Freedom	4.37	2.09	0.2289	0.7711
Freedom of the Press, Score	27.01	5.2	0.037	0.963
Internet users (per 100 people)	10.87	3.3	0.092	0.908
Press Freedom Index	8	2.83	0.125	0.875
Rule of Law	20.52	4.53	0.0487	0.9513
Government expenditure on education as % of GDP (%)	2.78	1.67	0.3591	0.6409
Language Fractionalization	4.57	2.14	0.2188	0.7812
Ethnic Fractionalization	4.51	2.12	0.2218	0.7782
Money Freedom	3.08	1.76	0.3244	0.6756

Table A5.3 Country list

High level democracy						*Low level democracy*	
AGO	EST	KOR	PRY	ALB	DOM	KEN	SLV
ARE	FIN	KWT	SAU	ARG	DZA	MAR	TUR
AUT	FJI	LBN	SGP	ARM	ECU	MDG	TZA
AZE	GAB	LBY	SVK	AUS	EGY	MEX	UGA
BEL	GEO	LKA	SVN	BEN	ESP	MLI	URY
BGR	GHA	LTU	SWE	BFA	GBR	MWI	USA
BHR	HND	LVA	SWZ	BGD	GIN	NGA	UZB
BLR	HRV	MDA	TCD	BOL	GRC	NOR	VEN
BLZ	HUN	MNG	THA	BRA	GTM	NPL	ZAF
BRB	IRL	MRT	TKM	CAN	HTI	NZL	ZMB
CHE	ISL	MUS	TTO	CHL	IDN	PER	SEN
CIV	JAM	NIC	TUN	CHN	IND	POL	JPN
CRI	JOR	NLD	UKR	CMR	IRN	PRT	DEU
CZE	KAZ	OMN	ZWE	COL	ISR	ROU	RUS
DNK	KGZ	PHL		CUB	ITA		

Notes

1 See http://info.worldbank.org/governance/wgi/pdf/ge.pdf.

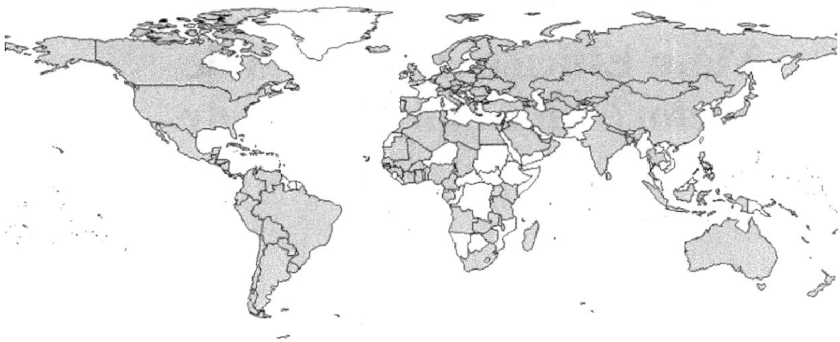

Figure A5.1 The coverage of sample countries

6 Are Democratic Countries More Efficient in the Public Sector? An Empirical Study with Cross-National Data

1 Introduction and Literature Background

Admit or not, the government is the most indispensable organization in modern countries. It controls many resources, collects incomes, and procures properties using authorized or non-authorized rights. According to World Development Indicators (World Bank, 2014), despite changes over the years, the average share of government final consumption expenditure in GDP around the world ranges from 15% to 18% since 1990, which is as large as 144.25% in Timor-Leste in 2001, and as small as 2.05% in Zimbabwe in 2008. Even in a pure market economy like Hong Kong, government expenditure accounts for 8.78% of GDP. Thus, the government is always there and plays a profound role in extensive aspects of residents' socio-economic life.

How to evaluate public sector efficiency (PSE) has attracted many research interests. Existing studies mainly measured and explained public sector efficiency using either data from local governments of specific countries/regions [e.g., Belgium (Van den Eeckaut et al., 1993), Spain (Balaguer-Coll et al., 2007), Finland (Loikkanen & Susiluoto, 2006), Minnesota, US (Hughes & Edwards, 2000), Portugal municipalities (Afonso & Fernandes, 2008), Chinese provinces (Chen & Zhang, 2008)] or data from country groups [e.g., EU new members and emerging markets (Afonso et al., 2010), OECD countries (Adam et al., 2011; Afonso & St. Aubyn, 2005), industrialized countries (Afonso et al., 2005) and developing countries (Grigoli & Kapsoli, 2013; Herrera & Pang, 2005)]. In this chapter, the authors built a cross-national dataset from both developing and developed countries. They employed the Data Envelopment Analysis (DEA) method to estimate and compare PSE among 117 countries.

Other researchers focus on institutions within a country such as fiscal autonomy (Boetti et al., 2012; Borge et al., 2008), budgetary transfers

DOI: 10.4324/9781003363712-6

and grants (Balaguer-Coll et al., 2007; Loikkanen & Susiluoto, 2006), and political factors such as governance quality, centralization of government power and party fragmentation (see Balaguer-Coll et al., 2007; Borge et al., 2008; Hughes & Edwards, 2000; Rayp & Van De Sijpe, 2007; Van den Eeckaut et al., 1993), this chapter focuses on the political regime's dynamics and quality. Despite many studies on the determinants of democracy (Acemoglu & Robinson, 2006; Barro, 1999) and the relationship between democracy and income or economic growth (Acemoglu et al., 2008; Gerring et al., 2005; Haan & Siermann, 1996; Leblang, 1996), few studies involved the relationship between democracy and efficiency of governments, especially at a cross-national level.

This chapter tries to bridge the gap in the existing literature by connecting political institutions with PSE with a cross-national dataset. One input and five output terms of public expenditure are developed with a series of sub-indicators. The two-stage DEA-Tobit method is used to estimate the political determinants of PSE. The first-stage estimation finds that there are two types of efficiency: the developing-country with low input and medium output, and the developed-country with high input and even higher output; the average score of PSEs in input-oriented measures is smaller than that in output-oriented, reflecting at least a 15% efficiency loss among 117 countries; high-income OECD countries, on average, have a better PSE than the rest of countries. The second-stage Tobit estimation shows that it is not the level of democracy but the persistence of political regimes that contributes to a better PSE; institutional quality regarding property rights protection and freedom from corruption takes a fundamental role in determining cross-national PSEs by shaping long-lasting political regimes.

The rest of the chapter is structured as follows. Section 2 introduces the empirical method, the construction of input and output terms for public expenditure, the explanatory variables of PSE, and data sources. Section 3 reports the score and rank of PSE for 117 countries. Section 4 presents the effects of the political system on PSE. Section 5 concludes the chapter.

2 Method, Data, and Variables

2.1 Method

Nonparametric DEA, other than Free Disposable Hull (FDH) or Stochastic Frontier Approach (SFA), is used in this chapter to estimate PSE across countries, although both FDH and SFA are broadly used in

PSE estimation (see, e.g., De Borger & Kerstens, 1996; Giménez & Prior, 2007; Grigoli & Kapsoli, 2013). PSE estimated from DEA, or FDH can lead to a direct result on the relative efficiency position of each decision unit, or how much output (input) can be increased (reduced) given current input (output) when they follow the best practice. A comparison study on the PSE estimated with DEA, FDH and SFA find that despite FDH on average produces larger PSE than SFA and DEA, PSEs obtained from different approaches are strongly correlated, and various methods provide consistent results on the efficiency rank of municipalities in Flanders (Geys & Moesen, 2009). De Borger and Kerstens (1996) also found in an empirical study on Belgian local governments that PSEs estimated from both two non-parametric methods (DEA and FDH) and three parametric methods (one deterministic and two stochastic) led to somewhat different levels of average efficiencies and rankings, but they produced similar results in the determinants of PSE.

The DEA method was developed by Charnes et al. (1978) based on the seminal work of Farrell (1957) to measure production efficiency with the input-output ratio. Compared with SFA, the non-parametric DEA method merits no specific assumptions on the production function. The behaviors of the decision-making unit (DMU) can be used in cases of multiple inputs and outputs. It does not require input or output prices in estimating efficiency frontiers and related measures of inefficiency. As a result, DEA has been broadly used in PSE estimations (e.g., Afonso & Fernandes, 2006; Afonso et al., 2010; Herrera & Pang, 2005; Hu & Edwards, 2000; Van den Eeckaut et al., 1993).

The DEA method by Charnes et al. (1978), i.e., the CCR model, assumes constant returns to scale concerning the frontier of technical efficiency. Since there is no reason to believe steady returns to scale for public expenditure, this chapter uses the DEA model developed by Banker et al. (1984), i.e., the BCC model, which allows for variable returns to scale, to estimate cross-national PSE. Both CCR and BCC models adopt linear programming to evaluate technical efficiency. The linear programming problem of the BCC model (Coelli, 1996) is given as follows:

$$\min_{\theta,\lambda} \theta$$

Subject to

$$\theta x_i - X\lambda \geq 0$$
$$Y\lambda \geq y_i$$
$$N1'\lambda = 1$$
$$\lambda \geq 0$$

where θ denotes the technical efficiency of DMU. When θ=1, the DMU is at the efficiency frontier; when θ<1, the DMU is not at the efficiency frontier, and $0 \leq \theta \leq 1$. X denotes the input matrix and Y denotes the output matrix. x_i and y_i denote the input and output vector of the ith DMU, respectively. λ is a nonnegative constant vector. N_1 is an $N \times 1$ vector of ones and $N_{1,}$ λ=1 is a convexity restriction on production frontier, i.e., the assumption of variable returns to scale. The BCC model envelops data much tighter than the CCR model, producing a scaling efficiency and more DMUs at the efficiency frontier.

Both input-oriented and output-oriented efficiency can be attained from the DEA model. The basic ideas of two kinds of measures can be simply illustrated in Figure 6.1 where the horizontal and vertical axes denote the amounts of input and output of DMUs, respectively. The black dots denote DMUs from A to G with respective input-output combinations. Measuring efficiency with the DEA method first involves identifying a production possibility frontier that envelopes data points assuming that the production possibility set is the smallest one satisfying convexity and free disposability and containing all observed input-output combinations (Banker et al., 1984). By this method, we can graph, in Figure 6.1, the production possibility frontier by connecting the input-output combinations of C, D, E, F, and G. Then, the efficiency is measured with the distance of some DMU to the constructed possibility frontier. Again in Figure 6.1, the input-oriented efficiency for DMU A is calculated as KJ/AJ, which reflects the input proportion of the potentially efficient amount, OH, to the actual amount used, OI, i.e., the relative efficiency of A to the production possibility frontier. Correspondingly, the output-oriented efficiency for DMU A is calculated as AI/LI, which reflects the output proportion of the actual amount used in the potentially efficient amount on the production possibility frontier. By taking similar procedures, we can also calculate the relative efficiency of DMU B.

Since not all factors influencing PSE are under the control of the government, the empirical studies further try to explain the PSEs from the first-stage estimation with demographic, political, or fiscal variables. This is termed the two-stage analysis of PSE. Since efficiency scores estimated in the first stage range from 0 to 1, they may not follow the Gaussian distribution. Direct use of the OLS method in the second stage may result in biased estimation. Thus, similar to existing literature (Afonso & Fernandes, 2008; Afonso et al., 2010; Rayp & Van De Sijpe, 2007), the Tobit model is used in the second-stage analysis to estimate the effect of democracy on cross-national PSE.

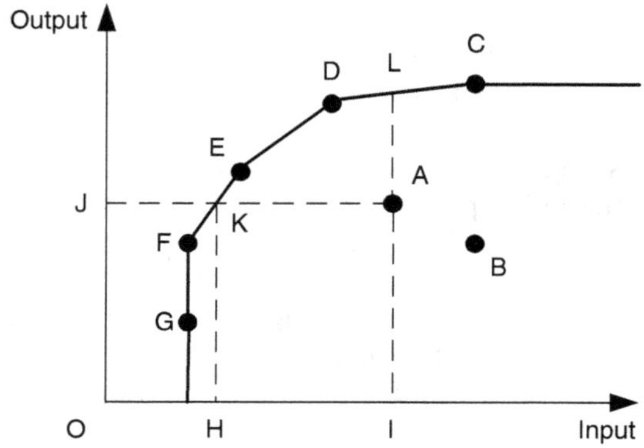

Figure 6.1 Input-oriented and output-oriented efficiency in a BCC model with one input and one output

Source: Own figure, based on Rayp and Van De Sijpe (2007): Figure 1

Other than the two-stage DEA-Tobit procedure, Adam et al. (2011) used a three-stage model which first uses DEA to get the gross PSE, then uses the SFA to separate efficiency of the macroeconomic environment and statistical noise from the gross PSE, and finally uses DEA method again to estimate PSE, but with inputs adjusted by the effects of nondiscretionary factors. As a result, PSEs estimated in the last stage are solely attributed to government managerial practices be pretty compared across countries. The results show that the three-stage method does not significantly change the PSE ranking among countries. PSE scores attained from different methods are highly correlated, indicating the robustness of the simple DEA method.[1] Considering that this chapter also aims to investigate the effect of democracy on PSE, the authors simply employ the DEA-Tobit procedure to estimate cross-national PSE and explain it with variables on political regimes.

2.2 Input and Output Terms of Public Expenditure

Based on existing empirical work (Adam et al., 2011; Afonso et al., 2005; Afonso & Fernandes, 2006; Chen & Zhang, 2008; Wu et al., 2010), the input of public expenditure is measured with the proportion of public spending to GDP.

However, the selection of output indicators in the existing literature is quite different. Both narrow and broad measures are used to proxy outputs of public expenditures. For example, when estimating the PSE of 51 Portuguese municipalities in Lisbon and Vale do Tejo, Afonso and Fernandes (2006) chose only four output indicators, i.e., general administration, education, social service, sanitation, and environment protection. Other empirical studies also consider narrow measures on public output (e.g., Borge et al., 2008; Geys & Moesen, 2009; Loikkanen & Susiluoto, 2006).

However, some other studies (e.g., Adam et al., 2011; Afonso et al., 2010) choose much broader measures because the government provides public goods and services and is responsible for macroeconomic performance. Thus, economic growth, unemployment, inflation, and income distribution are also included as output indicators of public expenditure.

Due to substantial socio-economic divergence and heterogeneity in public outputs among countries, narrow output measures might produce misleading results in PSEs. The authors adopt broad measures on general output. Based on the existing literature and the availability of the data, the output indicators are chosen as follows.

Public education output. This output is measured with the gross secondary school enrollment ratio. It is calculated as the ratio of the secondary-school enrollment to the population.

Public health output. In addition to two commonly used sub-indicators in the existing literature, i.e., life expectancy at birth and the inverse of infant mortality under five years old (Adam et al., 2011; Afonso et al., 2010; Rayp & Van De Sijpe, 2007), we also include the share of population covered by improved sanitation facilities like the health output.

Environment protection output. Two sub-indicators are selected to measure environment protection output: the percentage of forestry area in total land area and kilograms of CO_2 emissions per-capita GDP in PPP terms.

Public infrastructure output. This output includes three sub-indicators: the share of the population with access to a cleaned water source, the proportion of paved road length to total road length, and Internet users per thousand persons.

Macroeconomic performance output. This output includes four sub-indicators: the growth rate of GDP, unemployment rate, inflation rate, and economic stability measured with the standard deviation of GDP growth rate.

The input and outputs of public expenditures across countries are collected from the World Bank Open Data (World Bank, 2014). Adam et al. (2011) argued that it takes time for public inputs to produce public outputs. The potential business cycle in public investments can be excluded from the averaged data; the authors average all input and output indicators for each country from 2001 to 2010. Since the information is unavailable for all countries during the period, a ten-year averaged dataset for 117 countries is constructed to estimate the PSE.

Following existing studies (Afonso & Fernandes, 2006; Afonso et al., 2010; Chen & Zhang, 2008; Wu et al. 2010), all values of each sub-indicator are further normalized by first dividing them with the means of 117 countries and then by assigning each sub-indicator an equal weight to get five output indicators of public expenditure.[2] Moreover, for indicators such as CO2 emissions per-capita GDP in PPP terms, unemployment rate, inflation rate, and economic stability, in which a larger value denotes a lower output level, we use the reciprocals of their normalized indicators as the output values.

2.3 Determinants of Public Sector Efficiency

Existing studies first include demographic and economic variables such as the size of the jurisdiction, education, and income as the determinants of PSE (see, e.g., Afonso et al., 2010; Balaguer-Coll et al., 2007; Loikkanen & Susiluoto, 2006; Van den Eeckaut et al., 1993). In addition, poor governance quality, centralization of government power, votes of the governing party in total population, and party fragmentation are found adverse to PSE (see Balaguer-Coll et al., 2007; Borge et al., 2008; Hughes & Edwards, 2000; Rayp & Van De Sijpe, 2007; Van den Eeckaut et al., 1993). Considering both the aim of this chapter and the availability of the data at the cross-national level, we choose the following variables to explain the PSE across countries: GDP per capita, the share of public expenditure, resident education level, urbanization rate and population density, openness as well as some institutional variables regarding political regimes, fiscal freedom, and institutional quality.

The data on GDP per capita, the share of public expenditure, urbanization, population density, and openness are also collected from World Bank Open Data. The average years of resident education are taken from Barro and Lee (2013), who provided a comprehensive estimation of the average schooling years of adult residents across the world. Institutional variables contain the following variables:

(i) The level of democracy in a country. Compared with the monocratic regime, the democratic regime entitles residents with political rights to decide fiscal budget and expenditures, which might constrain the government's wastes in public spending and thus improve PSE. However, due to the dilemma of collective actions and complicated political decision procedures, democracy may also result in inefficient public resources.

Three sources of democracy indicators are used to measure the level of democracy in a country. The first one is taken from the Polity IV Project (2011), which provided a democracy indicator (i.e., Polity2 index) of 164 countries from 1800 to 2011. This indicator ranges from 10, full democracy, to -10, full monocracy. The second one is Freedom House (2015)'s Political Rights Indicator (PRI). PRI categorizes countries into seven groups according to the extent of political rights enjoyed by the resident, where group 1 consists of countries with the highest level of political rights. In contrast, group 7 consists of countries with the lowest level of political rights. These two indicators are broadly used in the existing literature to measure the level of democracy across the world (e.g., Acemoglu et al., 2008; Barro, 1999; Gerring et al., 2005). The third one is a dichotomous measure of democracy which divides countries into either democratic ones, which take a value of one, or monocracies, which take a value of zero. This indicator is taken from Boix (2003, pp. 98–109).

(ii) Regime durability. This variable measures the persistence of the current political regime. It consists of two indicators which are also taken from Polity IV Project. The first indicator, the durability of current regime, denotes "the number of years since the most recent regime change or the end of transition period defined by the lack of stable political institutions (page no. 17)" (Marshall et al., 2014). Since regime stability enables the government to adjust public expenditures for public needs, we expect that the higher durability of the current regime might enhance PSE. The second one, the durability of democracy, is a dummy variable. If a country took a democratic regime from 1950 to 2010, the variable would take the value of one. Otherwise, it would take the weight of zero. Based on the stock concept of democracy (Gerring et al., 2005) that it takes time for a democratic polity to generate enough political capital by learning and institutionalization and run effectively to provide public products and services, the authors expect that countries with as long as 60 years experience of a democratic regime have a higher PSE than others.

(iii) The other three institutional variables include property rights protection, freedom from corruption, and fiscal freedom. Since property rights are the foundation of a market economy, and a "good" institution provides stronger protection on property rights and prevents government corruption more effectively, the first two indicators can also measure institutional quality in a country.[3] Fiscal freedom measures the ability of a government to collect the public income. All indicators are borrowed from Economic Freedom Index (Heritage Foundation, 2012), with values ranging from 0 to 100 since 1995. The authors expect that institutional quality is positively associated with PSE, while fiscal freedom is negatively associated with PSE.

In accordance with indicators, all explanatory variables except the durability of democracy are averaged into a ten-year (2001–2010) cross-national dataset. The seven-category regional dummies by World Bank are also controlled because the unchanged geographical, cultural, or religious factors may influence PSE. Appendix Table A6.1 provides detailed information on the definition of all variables and data sources. Table 6.1 presents the descriptive statistics for all variables.

Table 6.1 Descriptive statistics

Variable	*Obs*	*Mean*	*Std. Dev.*	*Min*	*Max*
Input					
Public expenditure	117	15.868	4.873	5.187	27.980
Outputs					
Public education					
Primary schooling enrollments	117	102.808	12.264	44.877	134.336
Secondary schooling enrollments	117	78.425	27.500	9.576	138.277
Public health					
Life expectancy at birth	117	70.421	8.555	44.687	82.198
Infant mortality	117	35.897	41.149	3.055	209.609
Improved sanitation facilities	117	76.495	27.288	8.400	100
Environment protection					
Forest area	117	11.967	9.576	0.003	53.751
CO2 emission	117	0.418	0.291	0.029	1.439
Infrastructure					
Internet users	117	26.210	23.539	0.214	84.866
Paved roads	117	54.489	31.641	3.500	100

Variable	*Obs*	*Mean*	*Std. Dev.*	*Min*	*Max*
Improved water source	117	88.722	14.564	37.800	100
Macroeconomic performance					
GDP growth	117	4.068	2.282	–0.773	15.286
Unemployment	117	9.680	7.975	0.700	59.500
Inflation	117	5.917	4.599	–0.263	27.650
Stability	117	3.464	2.454	0.702	20.192
Nondiscretionary Factors					
Ln (GDP per capita)	92	8.935	1.161	6.439	11.126
Urbanization	92	58.957	21.302	12.393	98.190
Population density	92	109.200	114.489	1.660	613.160
Education	92	8.359	2.636	1.691	13.004
Openness	92	85.745	40.810	25.500	301.600
Institutions					
Polity2	92	0.778	0.273	0.15	1
Political Rights Index	89	2.876	1.999	1	7
Dichotomous democracy	92	0.761	0.429	0	1
Years of current regime	92	30.917	34.372	1.6	196.5
Democracy since 1950	92	0.228	0.422	0	1
Property rights	92	50.478	23.839	10	90.5
Freedom from corruption	92	43.827	22.369	10	96.4
Fiscal freedom	92	71.595	13.739	10	99.9

Data source: see Appendix Table A6.1.

3 Cross-National Public Sector Efficiency

The PSEs for 117 countries are estimated using the DEA method with input and output terms described above. Table 6.2 summarizes the efficiency scores and ranks of PSE in input-oriented and output-oriented measures. There are 14 and 15 efficiency frontiers in input-oriented and output-oriented measures, respectively, most of which are developed countries such as Australia, Belgium, Denmark, Germany, Iceland, Luxembourg, Norway, Sweden, and Switzerland. There are also frontiers from developing countries, including Afghanistan, Benin, Cambodia, Romania, and Vietnam. The output-oriented measure produces one more efficiency frontier, Uruguay. Table 6.2 also shows that countries with PSE scores ranking in the bottom ten are all developing countries.

Countries in East Asia and Pacific regions, on average, have higher efficiency scores than those in other regions. Nineteen OECD countries in our sample, on average, have the highest PSE among different country groups. On the contrary, underdeveloped countries in

Sub-Saharan Africa, Middle East, and North Africa regions have the lowest average PSE. Thus, high-income countries generally have a better PSE than those middle- and low-income countries. The mean of PSE in the input-oriented measures is 0.64, which is lower than that in the output-oriented measures, 0.853. The results indicate that if all countries follow the best practice, 36% of input can be saved without changing the current output produced, or about

Table 6.2 Summary on the scores and rank of public sector efficiency across countries

	Input-oriented efficiency (15 countries)	*Output-oriented efficiency (16 countries)*
Frontier countries	Australia, Belgium, Denmark, Germany, Iceland, Luxembourg, Norway, Sweden, Switzerland, Afghanistan, Benin, Cambodia, Romania, Vietnam	Australia, Belgium, Denmark, Germany, Iceland, Luxembourg, Norway, Sweden, Switzerland, Afghanistan, Benin, Cambodia, Romania, Vietnam, Uruguay
Countries ranking in the bottom ten	Djibouti, Mauritania, Suriname, West Bank and Gaza, Namibia, Burkina Faso, Iraq, Bhutan, Morocco, Macedonia	Djibouti, Mauritania, Iraq, Pakistan Yemen, Rep., Senegal, Sierra Leone, Ethiopia, Morocco, Ghana
Average efficiency score (standard deviation)		
East Asia & Pacific	0.768 (0.212)	0.911 (0.088)
Europe & Central Asia	0.688 (0.218)	0.895 (0.090)
Latin America & Caribbean	0.695 (0.181)	0.892 (0.069)
Middle East & North Africa	0.467 (0.131)	0.754 (0.164)
North America	0.616 (0.088)	0.888 (0.028)
South Asia	0.652 (0.226)	0.809 (0.150)
Sub-Saharan Africa	0.478 (0.173)	0.735 (0.126)
OECD	0.872 (0.162)	0.974 (0.038)
In total	0.640 (0.219)	0.853 (0.123)

Note: 19 OECD countries in the sample are Australia, Austria, Belgium, Canada, Switzerland, Germany, Denmark, Spain, Finland, France, United Kingdom, Ireland, Iceland, Japan, Luxembourg, Norway, Portugal, Sweden, and United States; Standard deviations in parentheses; the results are derived from DEAP version 2.1 developed by Coelli (1996).

15% of output can be increased without changing the current inputs. Appendix Table A6.2 presents the detailed scores and ranks of each country in our sample.

One may be surprised that efficiency frontiers also include some developing countries. Although developing countries have lower public expenditure outputs, they have an even lower public expenditure than developed countries, making some developing countries the efficiency frontiers in producing lower outcomes with much lower input. As a result, there are two efficiency frontiers: the developing-country frontiers, with fewer outputs using much less input. The developed-country frontiers use a more considerable input to produce even more outputs.

4 Institutional Factors and Public Sector Efficiency

4.1 Democracy and Public Sector Efficiency

We first examine the influence of the level of democracy on public sector efficiency using Tobit models. The results are reported in Table 6.3 where three alternative sources of democracy variables are used to test the effect of democracy on PSE in both input-oriented and output-oriented measures. The results show that despite changes in the indicators of democracy and measures of PSE, democracy fails to explain the difference in PSE among countries. Estimated coefficients of Polity 2, political rights, and dichotomous democracy are all statistically insignificant, although they are positive. Thus, not a simple relationship can be estimated between democracy and PSE.[4] Although political rights entitled by a democratic political system can prevent extreme misallocation of public resources by enhancing resident participation in the public decision-making process, they may not guarantee that public incomes are used efficiently. Besides, the long-lasting political procedures for fiscal budget imply some degree of inefficiency.

Among other variables, we can tell from Table 6.3 that GDP per capita, the share of public expenditure in GDP, and some region dummies produce a consistent influence on PSE. Larger GDP per capita and lower public spending will contribute to higher PSE in two measures. This is consistent with efficiency scores in Table 6.2 that developed countries account for more efficiency frontiers, and, on average, have higher PSEs than developing countries. The negative effect of public expenditure on PSE is because it is the only input of public sectors used to estimate PSE with the DEA method in the last part. In addition, urbanization is positively associated with input-oriented efficiency (see Models (1)–(3) of Table 6.3). An increase in the urbanization rate by 1% will increase input-oriented efficiency by at least 0.245 points.

In contrast to some earlier studies from specific countries (e.g., Loikkanen & Susiluoto, 2006; Van den Eeckaut et al., 1993), our study with cross-national data finds a negative effect of education on input-oriented efficiency (see also Models (1)–(3)). A one-year increase in resident education will reduce input-oriented efficiency scores by 2.036–2.505 points. This may be due to the increasing demand for education for public expenditure, which leads to a lower PSE in the input–output relationship. Although there is evidence that education can promote political participation (Milligan et al., 2004), this participation does not necessarily result in efficient public expenditure. It may increase public demands for government expenditure, enlarging governmental deficits in many developed countries.

Similar to Rapy and Van de Sijpe (2007)'s study on developing countries where Asian ones have a significantly higher PSE, we find remarkable regional differences in cross-national PSE. Compared with East Asia and Pacific region countries, countries in the Middle East, North Africa, North America, and Sub-Saharan Africa have significantly lower PSEs.

4.2 Regime Durability and Public Sector Efficiency

This section further tests if regime durability influences cross-national public sector efficiency based on the argument that political institutions require time to institutionalize and form political capital (Gerring et al., 2005). Two indicators are employed here to capture the time effect of the political system on PSE, i.e., persistent years of the current regime in either democracy or monocracy, and the duration of democracy. The Pearson correlation coefficient of the two variables is 0.735, implying a positive correlation between the two. Thus, we treat them as alternative variables other than complement variables of regime durability.[5] The results are presented in Table 6.4, where we can see that both indicators of regime durability are significantly and positively associated with the PSE in two measures.

Years of current regime contribute significantly to input-oriented and output-oriented efficiency with coefficients no less than 0.2 and 0.11, respectively. Coefficients in the reduced-form models (Models

Table 6.3 Democracy and public sector efficiency

	(1)	*(2)*	*(3)*	*(4)*	*(5)*	*(6)*
Variables	*Input-oriented efficiency*			*Output-oriented efficiency*		
Polity2	4.999			3.728		
	(9.821)			(6.034)		
Political rights		7.598			5.926	
		(9.019)			(5.588)	
Dichotomous democracy			–5.219			0.684
			(6.197)			(4.190)
Ln (GDP per capita)	10.995***	10.707***	11.046***	7.043***	6.329***	7.053***
	(2.448)	(2.542)	(2.542)	(1.550)	(1.470)	(1.457)
Public expenditure	–2.455***	–2.131***	–2.044***	–0.921***	–0.821**	–0.781**
	(0.556)	(0.558)	(0.576)	(0.321)	(0.324)	(0.333)
Urbanization	0.264**	0.245**	0.309**	0.024	0.035	0.047
	(0.127)	(0.114)	(0.127)	(0.088)	(0.073)	(0.081)
Population density	–0.004	–0.008	–0.008	0.001	–0.001	–0.005
	(0.020)	(0.009)	(0.019)	(0.009)	(0.005)	(0.009)
Education	–2.036*	–2.505**	–2.257*	–0.078	–0.388	–0.318
	(1.145)	(1.108)	(1.137)	(0.643)	(0.615)	(0.601)
Openness	–0.015	–0.017	–0.013	–0.028	–0.020	–0.018
	(0.053)	(0.053)	(0.056)	(0.030)	(0.031)	(0.031)
Europe & Central Asia	–6.555	–8.723	–7.184	–4.113	–4.601	–4.852
	(6.769)	(6.478)	(6.636)	(3.247)	(3.202)	(3.121)
Latin America & Caribbean	–17.266**	–19.520***	–16.403**	–6.468*	–7.727**	–7.185**

(Continued)

	(1)	(2)	(3)	(4)	(5)	(6)
Variables	*Input-oriented efficiency*			*Output-oriented efficiency*		
	(6.638)	(6.310)	(6.361)	(3.471)	(3.248)	(3.382)
Middle East & North Africa	–28.805***	–32.905***	–37.583***	–12.245**	–13.658***	–15.328***
	(7.575)	(7.589)	(8.215)	(4.744)	(4.741)	(5.141)
North America	–28.450***	–31.701***	–29.518***	–15.496***	–15.890***	–16.023***
	(8.989)	(7.439)	(8.666)	(4.196)	(3.644)	(3.951)
South Asia	–6.251	0.778	2.546	–11.599	–5.679	–4.373
	(10.040)	(12.694)	(12.599)	(8.633)	(9.520)	(9.536)
Sub-Saharan Africa	–16.265**	–21.357**	–17.910**	–9.647**	–12.531***	–11.174***
	(7.863)	(8.133)	(7.469)	(4.184)	(4.639)	(4.009)
Constant	17.937	23.434	20.497	43.019***	49.687***	44.792***
	(16.955)	(19.508)	(17.663)	(10.075)	(11.179)	(9.643)
Observations	92	95	95	92	95	95

Note: Robust standard errors are in parentheses; *, **, and *** denotes the significance level of 10%, 5%, and 1%, respectively; The reference region is East Asia and Pacific region; PSE scores are multiplied with 100, to make estimates easy to read.

(1) and (3)) are similar to those in the full models, which control other socio-economic variables (Models (2) and (4)). The results imply that the regime's stability can improve the PSE since political stability enables the government to provide efficient public goods and services over time. Given an average duration of 31 years of the current regime, years of the current regime, on average, increase input-oriented and output-oriented PSEs by more than 6 points and 3 points, respectively. A country with a regime lasting for 50 years will receive a 10-point higher input-oriented PSE and a 5.5-point higher output-oriented PSE.

Models (5)–(8) in Table 6.4 present the effects of democracy durability on PSE with different specifications. The results imply that countries with a persistent democratic regime since 1950 have a significantly better performance than other countries, i.e., at least 12.76 points higher in input-oriented PSE and 5.55 points higher in output-oriented PSE. We also see that coefficients are smaller when more explanatory variables are, but they all are statistically significant. Given the insignificant effect of democracy on PSE in Table 6.3, we find that stable democracy can lead to a higher PSE than the level of democracy itself. The results suggest one of the channels that the stock of democracy affects economic growth by providing more efficient public policies (Gerring et al., 2005).

4.3 The Role of Institutional Quality

Two variables, property rights protection and freedom from corruption, are used to examine the role of institutional quality in shaping the relationship between political systems and cross-national PSE. Table 6.5 presents Tobit results when variables on institutional quality and regime durability are controlled in the same Model. To avoid severe multi-collinearity, the two highly correlated institutional-quality variables (with Pearson correlation coefficients larger than 0.9) are put in different models.

Similar to Afonso et al. (2010), it can be seen that from Models (1)–(4) of Table 6.5, property rights protection produces statistically significant and positive influences on PSE in two measures. A 1-point increase in property rights protection will lead to an increase in the predicted value of PSE by about 0.3 in input-oriented measures and about 0.15 in output-oriented measures. Freedom from corruption also has significant and positive effects on PSE, and they are much larger than those caused by property rights protection (see Models (5)–(8)).

Table 6.4 Regime durability and public sector efficiency across countries

	(1)	*(2)*	*(3)*	*(4)*	*(5)*	*(6)*	*(7)*	*(8)*
Variables	*Input-oriented efficiency*		*Output-oriented efficiency*		*Input-oriented efficiency*		*Output-oriented efficiency*	
Years of current regime	0.205**	0.213**	0.113***	0.129***				
	(0.098)	(0.098)	(0.040)	(0.043)				
Democracy from 1950 to 2010					12.761**	19.850***	5.551**	8.160***
					(5.914)	(5.818)	(2.471)	(2.602)
Ln (GDP per capita)	4.995**	6.955**	4.771***	4.739***	3.600	6.095**	4.212***	4.809***
	(2.489)	(2.678)	(1.268)	(1.620)	(2.445)	(2.453)	(1.313)	(1.652)
Public expenditure		–2.623***		–1.027***		–2.430***		–0.899***
		(0.504)		(0.325)		(0.471)		(0.299)
Urbanization		0.345***		0.080		0.343***		0.085
		(0.129)		(0.077)		(0.124)		(0.076)
Population density		–0.015		–0.008		–0.019**		–0.005
		(0.018)		(0.009)		(0.008)		(0.004)
Education		–1.673*		0.106		–1.709*		–0.020
		(0.997)		(0.601)		(0.999)		(0.632)
Openness		0.013		–0.008		–0.016		–0.018
		(0.053)		(0.031)		(0.049)		(0.030)
Regional dummies	Yes	Yes	Yes	Yes	Yes	Yes	Yes	Yes
Constant	33.182	43.589**	49.215***	57.916***	50.173**	59.530***	56.985***	61.194***
	(23.327)	(18.308)	(11.487)	(10.474)	(23.466)	(18.493)	(12.152)	(11.984)
Observations	104	93	104	93	98	98	98	98

Note: Robust standard errors in parentheses; *, **, and *** denote significant levels of 10%, 5%, and 1%, respectively; PSE scores are multiplied by 100 to make estimates easy to read.

The coefficients of freedom from corruption are about 0.72 and 0.33 in input-oriented and output-oriented measures, respectively. Due to the strong quality effects of space from corruption on PSE, coefficients of the regime durability, which are previously significant in Table 6.4, i.e., years of current regime and democracy from 1950 to 2010, are now less significant (also see Models (5)–(8)). The results imply that reliable property rights and freedom from corruption are more critical than regime durability in improving PSE.

To investigate the crowding-out effect of institutional quality variables on the roles of other political variables in explaining global PSE, Table 6.6 further provides OLS results by regressing regime durability with property rights protection and freedom from corruption. After controlling for a series of potential determinants of the regime's durability, such as GDP growth rate, inflation rate, population density, openness, and region dummies, we found that both institutional quality variables are significantly and positively correlated with two measures of regime durability. A one-point improvement in property rights protection and freedom from corruption is associated with a one-year persistence of the current regime and a 1% larger probability of a democratic regime lasting over 60 years. Such effects are substantial considering the mean scores of property rights and freedom from corruption are 49.9 and 42.73, respectively, implying, on average, the two variables contribute to about 50 years persistence of the current regime and more than 50% chance to be a democratic country lasting for 60 years. Such a decisive role of institutional quality also renders the estimate of GDP per capita less significant. However, public expenditure remains a significant factor determining both measures of PSEs (see Table 6.5), which indicates that although the public cost is discretionary to the government, it should not be omitted in the second-stage analysis.[6]

Table 6.5 also shows that fiscal freedom significantly reduces PSE in input-oriented measures, not output-oriented measures. Here, budgetary freedom measures the tax burden faced by the government. A more considerable value in fiscal freedom implies a more powerful government and more considerable freedom for the government to use public income, resulting in a lower input-oriented PSE. The result is consistent with existing studies on specific countries, which find that fiscal freedom (autonomy) leads to lower PSE (Balaguer-Coll et al., 2007; Boetti et al., 2012; Borge et al., 2008).

Table 6.5 Institutional quality and public sector efficiency across countries

	(1)	*(2)*	*(3)*	*(4)*	*(5)*	*(6)*	*(7)*	*(8)*
Variables	*Input-oriented efficiency*		*Output-oriented efficiency*		*Input-oriented efficiency*		*Output-oriented efficiency*	
Years of current regime	0.103		0.102**		0.002		0.060	
	(0.086)		(0.045)		(0.085)		(0.042)	
Democracy since 1950		11.588**		5.437**		3.988		2.063
		(5.209)		(2.518)		(4.721)		(2.402)
Property rights	0.327***	0.281***	0.147**	0.146**				
	(0.120)	(0.101)	(0.071)	(0.067)				
Freedom from corruption					0.749***	0.694***	0.330***	0.334***
					(0.154)	(0.143)	(0.086)	(0.085)
Fiscal freedom	–0.445**	–0.309*	–0.054	–0.019	–0.363**	–0.263*	–0.021	0.003
	(0.199)	(0.180)	(0.111)	(0.107)	(0.153)	(0.141)	(0.093)	(0.089)
Ln (GDP per capita)	3.425	3.583	3.178*	3.540**	–1.633	–1.609	0.990	1.165
	(2.721)	(2.733)	(1.818)	(1.779)	(2.998)	(2.851)	(2.030)	(1.931)
Public expenditure	–3.553***	–3.045***	–1.232***	–1.043***	–3.853***	–3.379***	–1.372***	–1.201***
	(0.504)	(0.521)	(0.346)	(0.330)	(0.492)	(0.531)	(0.345)	(0.339)
Urbanization	0.260**	0.254**	0.040	0.042	0.187*	0.177	0.008	0.007
	(0.115)	(0.118)	(0.083)	(0.077)	(0.108)	(0.106)	(0.078)	(0.070)
Population density	–0.016	–0.020**	–0.006	–0.005	–0.001	–0.005	0.000	0.002
	(0.015)	(0.007)	(0.008)	(0.004)	(0.013)	(0.007)	(0.008)	(0.004)

	(1)	(2)	(3)	(4)	(5)	(6)	(7)	(8)
Variables	*Input-oriented efficiency*		*Output-oriented efficiency*		*Input-oriented efficiency*		*Output-oriented efficiency*	
Education	–0.646	–0.879	0.452	0.266	–0.311	–0.401	0.605	0.493
	(1.004)	(1.021)	(0.670)	(0.690)	(0.979)	(0.955)	(0.674)	(0.672)
Openness	–0.008	–0.037	–0.028	–0.038	–0.014	–0.036	–0.031	–0.037
	(0.044)	(0.045)	(0.027)	(0.027)	(0.040)	(0.042)	(0.026)	(0.026)
Regional dummies	Yes	Yes	Yes	Yes	Yes	Yes	Yes	Yes
Constant	105.532***	100.639***	73.387***	71.318***	133.661***	129.102***	85.731***	84.227***
	(25.714)	(24.338)	(16.482)	(16.294)	(25.337)	(24.138)	(17.064)	(16.683)
Observations	92	97	92	97	92	97	92	97

Note: Robust standard errors in parentheses; *, **, and *** denote the significant level of 10%, 5%, and 1%, respectively; PSE scores are multiplied by 100, to make estimates easy to read.

Table 6.6 Institutional quality and regime durability

	(1)	*(2)*	*(3)*	*(4)*
Variables	*Years of current regime*		*Democracy since 1950*	
Property rights protection	0.976***		0.011***	
	(0.220)		(0.002)	
Freedom from corruption		1.244***		0.014***
		(0.195)		(0.002)
GDP growth	0.960	1.968	–0.004	0.005
	(1.580)	(1.350)	(0.024)	(0.025)
Population density	0.002	0.024	0.000**	0.001***
	(0.028)	(0.022)	(0.000)	(0.000)
Inflation rate	–0.054	0.423	0.005	0.009
	(0.547)	(0.469)	(0.007)	(0.007)
Openness	–0.084	–0.080	–0.000	0.000
	(0.076)	(0.070)	(0.001)	(0.001)
Region dummies	Yes	Yes	Yes	Yes
Constant	–8.622	–22.142*	–0.327*	–0.436**
	(12.142)	(13.276)	(0.182)	(0.166)
Observations	92	92	97	97
R-squared	0.412	0.502	0.523	0.578

Note: Robust standard errors in parentheses; *, ** and *** denote significant level of 10%, 5% and 1%, respectively. PSE scores are multiplied by 100, to make estimates easy to read.

5 Conclusion

This chapter employs the two-stage DEA-Tobit method to estimate and explain PSE with institution variables. One input and five outputs of public expenditure are constructed to measure PSE in the first-stage DEA estimation. Two types of efficiency frontiers are produced: the developing country frontiers and the developed country frontiers. However, on average, governments in developed countries perform better than those in developing countries because the former has more efficiency frontiers and fewer countries with inferior performance. By following the best practice, 36% (15) of input (outputs), on average, can be saved (increased) without changing the current amounts of outputs (input).

The second-stage analysis with Tobit models first finds that no significant relationship exists between democracy and PSE at the cross-national level, implying that the level of democracy is not necessarily relevant to PSE. However, we find strong evidence that the durability of the current regime and stable democracy contribute to improving cross-national PSE by providing high-quality institutions that can offer strong property rights protection and freedom from corruption.

Our findings suggest that it is not the level of democracy, but the stock of democracy contributes to cross-national PSEs. Whether democratic or monocratic, political regimes can be sustained by high-quality institutions with strong property rights protection and freedom from corruption. Thus, the results indicate that institutional quality matters more than democracy itself in determining cross-national PSE. Nevertheless, since democracy has been proven to provide better property rights protection than monocracy (Gradstein, 2007; Knutsen, 2011; Leblang, 1996), and a democratic regime tends to last longer, our results also suggest an indirect contribution of democracy on global PSE.

Notes

1 The Spearman correlation coefficients between the scores of public sector efficiency using three-stage estimation and those using only one-stage estimation are basically larger than 0.85, according to Adam et al. (2011)'s Table 2.
2 Despite change in the weight of sub-indicators, Afonso et al. (2005) found that rank correlations are in the (0.96 0.99) for PSE indicators.
3 Gradstein (2007) exemplified property rights protection as one of the indicators of institutional quality, where he also quoted, in the note, Adam Smith's sentences, emphasizing the importance of property rights protection, "In all countries where there is a tolerable security, every man of common understanding will endeavor to employ whatever stock he can command."
4 We also noted that if democracy is the only independent variable, the coefficients are statistically significant. However, there is no reason to assume that democracy is the only variable determining cross-national PSEs. Even if we employed the reduced-form model proposed by Gerring et al. (2005) that include only the logarithm of GDP per capita and regional dummies as additional control variables, all coefficients of democracy indicators are insignificant.
5 If both variables are controlled in the same model, both coefficients are insignificant while the Wald test for joint significance of both coefficients rejects the null hypothesis that they all equal to 0, which implies multi-collinearity in the model.
6 By similar OLS regressions in Table 6.6, we found that both variables are significantly associated with GDP per capita and the relationship is robust to the change of control variables.

References

Acemoglu, D., Johnson, S., Robinson, J. A., & Yared, P. (2008). Income and democracy. *American Economic Review, 98*, 808–842. doi:10.1257/aer.98.3.808

Acemoglu, D., & Robinson, J. A. (2006). *Economic origins of dictatorship and democracy*. New York: Cambridge University Press.

Adam, A., Delis, M., & Kammas, P. (2011). Public sector efficiency: Leveling the playing field between OECD countries. *Public Choice, 146*, 163–183. doi:10.1007/s11127-009-9588-7

Afonso, A., & Fernandes, S. (2006). Measuring local government spending efficiency: Evidence for the Lisbon region. *Regional Studies, 40*, 39–53. doi:10.1080/00343400500449937

Afonso, A., & Fernandes, S. (2008). Assessing and explaining the relative efficiency of local government. *Journal of Socio-Economics, 37*, 1946–1979. doi:10.1016/j.socec.2007.03.007

Afonso, A., Schuknecht, S., & Tanzi, V. (2005). Public sector efficiency: An international comparison. *Public Choice, 123*, 321–347. doi:10.1007/s11127-005-7165-2

Afonso, A., Schuknecht, L., & Tanzi, V. (2010). Public sector efficiency: Evidence for new EU member states and emerging markets. *Applied Economics, 42*, 2147–2164. doi:10.1080/00036840701765460

Afonso, A., & St. Aubyn, M. (2005). Non-parametric approaches to education and health efficiency in OECD countries. *Journal of Applied Economics, VIII*, 227–246.

Balaguer-Coll, M. T., Prior, D., & Tortosa-Ausina, E. (2007). On the determinants of local government performance: A two-stage nonparametric approach. *European Economic Review, 51*, 425–451.

Banker, R. D., Charnes, A., & Cooper, W. W. (1984). Some models for estimating technical and scale inefficiencies in data envelopment analysis. *Management Science, 30*, 1078–1092.

Barro, R. J. (1999). Determinants of democracy. *Journal of Political Economy, 107*, S158–S183.

Barro, R. J., & Lee, J. W. (2013). A new data set of educational attainment in the world, 1950–2010. *Journal of Development Economics, 104*, 184–198. doi:10.1016/j.jdeveco.2012.10.001

Boetti, L., Piacenza, M., & Turati, G. (2012). Decentralization and local governments' performance: How does fiscal autonomy affect spending efficiency? *FinanzArchiv Public Finance Analysis, 68*, 269–302. doi:10.1628/001522112X653840

Boix, C. (2003). *Democracy and redistribution*. Cambridge, UK: Cambridge University Press.

Borge, L. E., Falch, T., & Tovmo, P. (2008). Public sector efficiency: The roles of political and budgetary institutions, fiscal capacity, and democratic participation. *Public Choice, 136*, 475–495. doi:10.1007/s11127-008-9309-7

Charnes, A., Cooper, W. W., & Rhodes, E. (1978). Measuring the efficiency of decision making units. *European Journal of Operational Research, 2*, 429–444.

Chen, S., & Zhang, J. (2008). Efficiency of local government financial expenditure in China: 1978–2005 (in Chinese). *Social Sciences in China, 4*, 65–78.

Coelli, T. (1996). *A guide to DEAP Version 2.1: A data envelopment analysis (computer) program*. CEPA Working Paper 96/08.

De Borger, B., & Kerstens, K. (1996). Cost efficiency of Belgian local governments: A comparative analysis of FDH, DEA, and econometric approaches. *Regional Science and Urban Economics, 26*, 145–170.

Farrell, M. J. (1957). The measurement of productive efficiency. *Journal of the Royal Statistical Society Series A, 120*, 253–290.

Freedom House. (2015). *Freedom in the world* [WWW document]. https://freedomhouse.org/report-types/freedom-world#.VP2sM9IaY14

Gerring, J., Bond, P., Barndt, W. T., & Moreno, C. (2005). Democracy and economic growth: A historical perspective. *World Politics, 57*, 323–364. http://doi.org/10.1353/wp.2006.0002

Geys, B., & Moesen, W. (2009). Measuring local government technical (in) efficiency: An application and comparison of FDH, DEA, and econometric approaches. *Public Performance & Management Review, 32*, 499–513. doi:10.2753/PMR1530-9576320401

Giménez, V. M., & Prior, D. (2007). Long- and short-term cost efficiency frontier evaluation: Evidence from Spanish local governments. *Fiscal Studies, 28*, 121–139.

Gradstein, M. (2007). Inequality, democracy and the protection of property rights. *The Economic Journal, 117*, 252–269. doi:10.1111/j.1468-0297.2007.02010.x

Grigoli, F., & Kapsoli, J. (2013). *Waste not, want not: The efficiency of health expenditure in emerging and developing economies*. IMF Working Papers. doi:10.5089/9781484364260.001

Haan, J., & Siermann, C. L. J. (1996). New evidence on the relationship between democracy and economic growth. *Public Choice, 86*, 175–198.

Heritage Foundation. (2012). *Index of economic freedom* [WWW document]. http://www.heritage.org/index/country/vanuatu

Herrera, S., & Pang, G. (2005). *Efficiency of public spending in developing countries: An efficiency frontier.* World Bank Policy Research Working Paper 3645.

Hughes, N. P. A., & Edwards, M. E. (2000). Leviathan vs. Lilliputian: A data envelopment analysis of government efficiency. *Journal of Regional Science, 40*, 649–669.

Knutsen, C. H. (2011). Democracy, dictatorship and protection of property rights. *The Journal of Developmental Studies*. doi:10.1080/00220388.2010.506919

Leblang, D. A. (1996). Property rights, democracy and economic growth. *Political Research Quarterly, 49*, 5–26. doi:10.1177/106591299604900102

Loikkanen, H. A., & Susiluoto, I. (2006). *Cost efficiency of Finnish municipalities in basic service provision 1994–2002*. Helsinki Center of Economic Research Discussion Paper No. 96.

Marshall, M. G., Jaggers, K., & Gurr, T. R. (2014). *Polity IV Project: Dataset users' manual, v.2013*. Polity IV Project. doi:10.1177/0738894213499673

Milligan, K., Moretti, E., & Oreopoulos, P. (2004). Does education improve citizenship? Evidence from the United States and the United Kingdom. *Journal of Public Economics, 88*, 1667–1695.

Polity IV Project. (2011). *Regime authority characteristics and transitions datasets, 1800–2010* [WWW document]. http://www.systemicpeace.org/inscrdata.html

Rayp, G., & Van De Sijpe, N. (2007). Measuring and explaining government efficiency in developing countries. *The Journal of Developmental Studies, 43*, 360–381.

Van den Eeckaut, P., Tulkens, H., & Jamar, M.-A. (1993). Cost efficiency in Belgian municipalities. In H. Fried, C. Lovell, & S. Schmidt (Eds.), *The measurement of productive efficiency: Techniques and applications* (pp. 300–334). New York: Oxford University Press.

World Bank. (2014). *World Bank open data* [WWW document]. http://data.worldbank.org/

Wu, J.-H., Liu, C.-C., & Feng, Y.-Y. (2010). An empirical study of measuring public expenditure efficiency in Taiwan's local governments (in Chinese). *Public Administration and Policy, 50*, 33–80.

Appendix II

Table A6.1 Definition of variables and data source

Variables	*Definition*	*Data source*
Input		
public expenditure	% of government expenditure to GDP	Word Bank Open Data
Outputs		
Public education		Word Bank Open Data
Primary schooling enrollments	School enrollment, primary (% gross)	
Secondary schooling enrollments	School enrollment, secondary (% gross)	
Public health		Word Bank Open Data
Life expectancy	Life expectancy at birth, total (years)	
Infant mortality	Mortality rate, under 5 (per 1,000)	
Improved sanitation facilities	% of population with access to improved sanitation facilities.	
Environmental protection		Word Bank Open Data
Forest area	% of total land area	
CO2 emissions	kg per 2005 US $ of GDP	
Infrastructure		Word Bank Open Data
Improved water source	% of population with access to improved water source	
Paved roads	% of total roads	
Internet users	% of Internet users to total population	

(*Continued*)

Variables	*Definition*	*Data source*
Macroeconomic performance		
GDP growth	Growth rate of GDP, PPP (constant 2005 US $)	Word Bank Open Data
Unemployment	Unemployment, total (% of total labor force)	Word Bank Open Data
Inflation	CPI inflation rate, %	Word Bank Open Data
Stability	The standard deviation of GDP growth rate.	Author's calculation
Nondiscretionary factors		
GDP per capita	GDP per capita, PPP (constant 2005 US$)	Word Bank Open Data
Education	Average years of education for adults (age≥15).	Barro and Lee (2013)
Urbanization	Urban population (% of total)	Word Bank Open Data
Population density	People per sq. km of land area	
Openness	% of trade to GDP	
Institutions		
Polity2	Ranging from 10 (full democracy) to –10 (full monocracy). Normalized into values ranging from 1 to 0.	Polity IV Project
Political Rights Index	Political right indicator ranging from 1 (highest political rights) to 7 (lowest political rights). Normalized into values ranging from 1 to 0.	Freedom House
Dichotomous democracy	A dummy variable: 1 denotes democracy; 0 denotes monocracy.	Boix (2003, pp. 98–109)

Variables	*Definition*	*Data source*
Durability of current regime	Years of current regime.	Polity IV Project.
Durability of democracy	Democracy of a country since 1950.	
Property rights	The extent of property rights protection, a positive indicator ranging from 0 to 100, denoting without to full property rights protection.	The Wall Street Journal and the Heritage Foundation.
Freedom from corruption	The extent of a country free from corruption, ranging from 0 to 100, denoting complete corruption to full freedom from corruption.	
Fiscal freedom	Tax burden imposed by government, ranging from 0 to 100 denoting no fiscal freedom to full fiscal freedom.	
Region dummies	East Asia & Pacific, Europe & Central Asia, Latin America & Caribbean, Middle East & North Africa, North America, South Asia, Sub-Saharan Africa.	Word Bank Open Data

Table A6.2 Efficiency scores and ranks of public expenditure

Country	*Input-oriented*		*Output-oriented*		*Country*	*Input-oriented*		*Output-oriented*	
	Score	*Rank*	*Score*	*Rank*		*Score*	*Rank*	*Score*	*Rank*
Afghanistan	1	1	1	1	Korea, Rep.	0.826	27	0.956	27
Albania	0.769	34	0.923	40	Kuwait	0.68	46	0.963	24
Algeria	0.567	65	0.838	71	Kyrgyz Rep.	0.416	101	0.746	102
Antigua and Barbuda	0.636	54	0.884	51	Lao PDR	0.954	19	0.987	19
Armenia	0.743	37	0.918	41	Latvia	0.511	80	0.872	53
Australia	1	1	1	1	Lithuania	0.51	82	0.859	62
Austria	0.633	55	0.945	32	Luxembourg	1	1	1	1
Azerbaijan	0.641	53	0.885	50	Macedonia	0.367	108	0.724	105
Bahamas	0.831	26	0.942	34	Madagascar	0.557	66	0.815	77
Barbados	0.718	42	0.934	36	Malawi	0.433	98	0.774	92
Belgium	1	1	1	1	Malaysia	0.729	41	0.793	86
Belize	0.573	64	0.861	60	Mali	0.679	47	0.776	91
Benin	1	1	1	1	Malta	0.494	85	0.864	59
Bhutan	0.339	110	0.784	88	Mauritania	0.238	116	0.471	116
Bolivia	0.596	61	0.856	64	Mauritius	0.551	68	0.817	75
Bosnia and Herzegovina	0.438	95	0.801	81	Mexico	0.772	33	0.927	39
Botswana	0.449	94	0.883	52	Moldova	0.399	102	0.743	103
Bulgaria	0.529	73	0.814	78	Mongolia	0.537	70	0.823	73
Burkina Faso	0.289	112	0.688	107	Morocco	0.351	109	0.667	109
Cambodia	1	1	1	1	Namibia	0.283	113	0.758	100
Cameroon	0.536	72	0.782	89	Nepal	0.761	36	0.853	65

Country	*Input-oriented*		*Output-oriented*		*Country*	*Input-oriented*		*Output-oriented*	
	Score	*Rank*	*Score*	*Rank*		*Score*	*Rank*	*Score*	*Rank*
Canada	0.554	67	0.868	54	Nicaragua	0.934	20	0.976	22
Chile	0.802	31	0.935	35	Niger	0.434	97	0.71	106
China	0.488	86	0.853	66	Norway	1	1	1	1
Costa Rica	0.662	50	0.908	47	Pakistan	0.641	52	0.565	114
Croatia	0.503	83	0.819	74	Panama	0.61	60	0.848	68
Cyprus	0.683	45	0.904	48	Paraguay	0.691	44	0.885	49
Czech Rep.	0.536	71	0.867	55	Peru	0.958	18	0.986	20
Denmark	1	1	1	1	Philippines	0.822	28	0.944	33
Djibouti	0.199	117	0.382	117	Portugal	0.731	40	0.932	37
Dominica	0.885	22	0.981	21	Romania	1	1	1	1
Dominican Republic	0.886	21	0.959	25	Russian Federation	0.463	90	0.762	97
Ecuador	0.658	51	0.866	56	Senegal	0.425	99	0.574	112
Egypt	0.587	63	0.847	69	Serbia	0.421	100	0.772	93
El Salvador	0.627	57	0.845	70	Sierra Leone	0.475	88	0.603	111
Estonia	0.595	62	0.851	67	Slovak Republic	0.512	79	0.865	57
Ethiopia	0.373	106	0.606	110	Slovenia	0.84	25	0.951	31
Fiji	0.511	81	0.796	84	South Africa	0.458	92	0.792	87
Finland	0.996	16	0.999	16	Spain	0.806	29	0.959	26
France	0.763	35	0.989	18	Sri Lanka	0.674	49	0.909	45
Georgia	0.436	96	0.763	96	Suriname	0.265	115	0.752	101
Germany	1	1	1	1	Sweden	1	1	1	1
Ghana	0.468	89	0.674	108	Switzerland	1	1	1	1

(*Continued*)

Country	*Input-oriented*		*Output-oriented*		*Country*	*Input-oriented*		*Output-oriented*	
	Score	*Rank*	*Score*	*Rank*		*Score*	*Rank*	*Score*	*Rank*
Grenada	0.869	23	0.952	30	Syria	0.518	77	0.797	83
Guatemala	0.699	43	0.864	58	Tonga	0.772	32	0.93	38
Guyana	0.368	107	0.762	98	Trinidad and Tobago	0.627	56	0.86	61
Honduras	0.454	93	0.794	85	Tunisia	0.528	74	0.8	82
Hungary	0.46	91	0.817	76	Turkey	0.625	59	0.856	63
Iceland	1	1	1	1	Uganda	0.488	86	0.778	90
India	0.497	84	0.742	104	Ukraine	0.518	76	0.807	80
Indonesia	0.74	38	0.916	42	United Kingdom	0.625	58	0.973	23
Iran	0.547	69	0.833	72	United States	0.678	48	0.908	46
Iraq	0.314	111	0.565	115	Uruguay	0.999	15	1	1
Ireland	0.802	30	0.954	29	Vanuatu	0.394	103	0.761	99
Israel	0.513	78	0.91	44	Venezuela	0.735	39	0.916	43
Jamaica	0.527	75	0.814	79	Vietnam	1	1	1	1
Japan	0.981	17	0.994	17	West Bank and Gaza	0.27	114	0.769	94
Jordan	0.388	105	0.767	95	Yemen, Rep.	0.388	104	0.571	113
Kazakhstan	0.868	24	0.954	28	Mean	0.640		0.853	

7 Small Is Beautiful

Fighting Poverty with Low-Input-Technology in China Rural Area

Fighting poverty through concerted efforts and brainstorming is a key task for the sustainable development of the international community (Bapna, 2012). Different countries have their own experience and achieved remarkable results. Just around 30 years before, China together with India, Nigeria, Congo (DRC), Ethiopia, Bangladesh, and Tanzania accounted for 67% of the world's extremely poor population. Despite that, in 2020, China has achieved its poverty alleviation goal set in the *2030 Agenda for Sustainable Development* 10 years ahead of schedule, and nearly 100 million poor people have been lifted out of poverty, accounting for over 70% of global poverty reduction accomplishments over four decades, according to the World Bank's international poverty line standard.

On February 25, 2021, China announced that it had made great breakthrough in eradicating absolute poverty in eight years (The State Council Information Office of the People's Republic of China, 2021). Since 2013, the average poverty reduction speed in China has exceeded 10 million people per year, and the per capita disposable income of farmers in 832 impoverished counties has increased by about 10%. China's poverty reduction achievements have made outstanding contributions toward reducing world's poverty and the *Sustainable Development Goals.*

The technology know-how behind this proud transcript of China's targeted poverty alleviation is very compelling. Agricultural technology is the primary productive force, key to stimulating the vitality of agricultural and rural development, and to promoting agriculture modernization and rural poverty relief (Kassie et al., 2011). There are 200 million peasants in China carrying out smallholder production, and the number is 100 times bigger than that of the United States. Although China is currently developing technologies such as big data-based 5G smart agriculture, the best functional tool in China's

DOI: 10.4324/9781003363712-7

poverty reduction for now is not high agricultural technology but the low-input-technology or small technology to improve farmers' lives.

Those successful small technological tools share some distinct characteristics, such as low-cost (or zero-cost), easy-to-use interface and low threshold of access for technologically underprivileged farmers, no need for continuous investment from the state but lifelong benefits for farmers, and the embedding of modern concepts. The simpler an agricultural technology is, the easier it is for farmers to learn and apply it to planting practice, and the less the time and efforts they have to spend. For example, organic fertilizer, reasonably dense planting, greenhouse, insect proof net and weed eradication, etc. Obviously, only after the agricultural science and technology in the hands of scientists are mastered and applied by farmers can the effect of agricultural support and poverty reduction be brought into play (Figure 7.1).

As early as 1986, China explored and began to carry out poverty-relief tasks through science and technology. Over the past 30 years, a

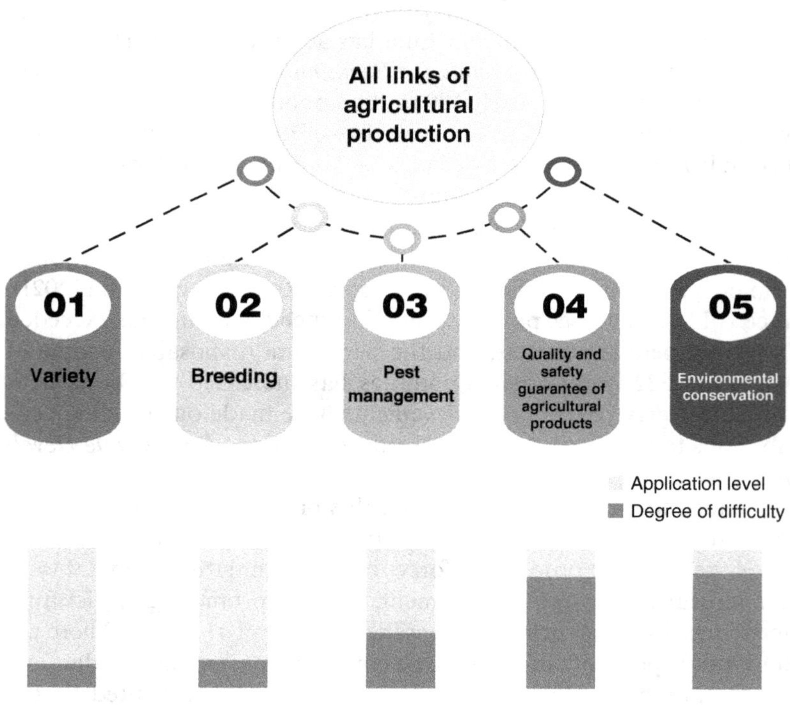

Figure 7.1 Application of low-input-technology in all links of agricultural production

large number of scientific and technological practitioners have gone deep into China's poor areas, where they have targeted the transfer of scientific and technological achievements and strengthened farmers' technical skills training. A variety of technology-oriented poverty-alleviation activities have been carried out, and innovative experience has been piloted nationwide. In China, it has to be mentioned that an important measure to use low-input technology to reduce poverty is the implementation of a science and technology commissioner policy, which originated in Nanping City, Fujian Province, China. This is a novel strategy to meet the basic technical needs of farmers.

Since 2002, researchers, technicians, and college students from scientific research institutes, with the support of government departments, have spread agricultural knowledge to farmers in a form that suits local context. At present, there are more than 800,000 scientific and technological commissioner throughout the country who are active at the grassroots level in rural areas, directly helping more than 65 million farmers and founding more than 30,000 scientific and technological enterprises.

In 2006, the United Nations Development Program supported the China Science and Technology Commissioner System to provide Chinese farmers with environmentally friendly agricultural technology and promote China's sustainable development. At the same time, China's science and technology commissioner system is gradually being promoted overseas. It offers technological assistance to South Asia and Southeast Asia and helps with their recruitment of national scientific and technological commissioners.

For example, the China Agricultural University has been cooperating with Tanzania to launch a campaign for science and technology commissioners since 2011 (Tanzania's version of campaign of special dispatch of science and technology). The professors from China taught farmers how to determine the planting density with the help of the cost-free hemp rope common in local areas. The agricultural technical commissioner has worked with local departments to formulate a technology promotion plan and teaches local farmers the high-yield corn planting technology through lectures, hands-on demonstrations, and field surveys (Zhang et al., 2016). More than 1,000 farmers have achieved a two to three times increase in grain production through reasonable dense planting, timely sowing and weeding, and shared these small technologies in more than ten villages in Tanzania.

In summary, in order to achieve the United Nations 2030 Sustainable Development Goals, governments, non-governmental organizations, and international organizations need to pay attention to small easy technologies that are of great significance to support rural and underdeveloped areas.

References

Bapna, M. (2012). World poverty: Sustainability is key to development goals. *Nature, 489*, 367.

Kassie, M., Shiferaw, B., & Muricho, G. (2011). Agricultural technology, crop income, and poverty alleviation in Uganda. *World Development, 39*(10), 1784–1795.

The State Council Information Office of the People's Republic of China. (2021). Full Text: Poverty Alleviation: China's Experience and Contribution. November 23, 2021, accessed at http://www.scio.gov.cn/zfbps/ndhf/44691/Document/1701663/1701663.htm.

Zhang, Y., Zheng, Y., Liu, Z., Li, Q., & Jingyi, Z. (2016). Technical promotion and poverty reduction: A review of China's efforts in Africa. *Annals of Agricultural & Crop Sciences, 1*, 1010–1012.

Index

Note: **Bold** page numbers refer to tables; *Italic* page numbers refer to figures and page numbers followed by "n" denote endnotes.

Adam, A. 130, 147n1
adaptability 2, 22, 33, 77
adaptive governance 15, 33–34
administrative authority 4, 26
administrative reforms 53, 54; Anglo-Saxon reform 57; developed Western countries 55; different perspectives **56**; former Soviet Union 55
administrative system 1, 3, 37; contracting system 3; improvement of 6; management power 7; performance 85; reform 7
Afonso, A. 131, 141, 147n2
Agenda for Sustainable Development 157
agricultural development 157; agricultural knowledge 159; low-input-technology 158, *158*; organic fertilizer 158
AHP *see* Analytic Hierarchy Process (AHP)
Almond, Gabriel 64
America's interstate relationships 65
Analytic Hierarchy Process (AHP) 67, *67*
Anglo-Saxon reform 57
Announcements of the State Council (ASC) 61, 62
anti-corruption 35
anti-poverty 49
Arab spring 75
ASC *see* Announcements of the State Council (ASC)
Asian economic crisis in 1997 31
authoritarianism 77
authoritarian regime 75
authoritarian rule 33
authority 23

Barro, R. J. 132
BCC model 128
belief systems 60
Benedict, Ruth 64
Borghans, L. 99
borrowing theory 60
bottom-up policy 15, 23
Breslin, Shaun G. 24
Bresnahan, T. F. 99
Buchanan, James 57
Buckley, Chris 50n2
budgetary system 11
budget revenue 11
bureaucratic championship system theory 18
bureaucratic corruption 80
bureaucratic operations 6
bureaucratic organization 42
bureaucratic systems 5, 20, 31, 66, 85
"buzzword" 30

cadre team building 5
campaign-oriented governance 20
CCDI *see* Central Commission for Discipline Inspection (CCDI)
censorship 73, 75; in authoritarian states 75; information censorship 74, 77, 88; Internet censorship 76, 83

Central Commission for Discipline Inspection (CCDI) 6, 38
central government 1; campaign-oriented governance 20; decentralization incentives 3; decision-maker 2; economic power 6; governing officials 3; human resources management 5; laissez-faire attitude 16; management of 2
centralization 4, 10, 17, 19; combination of 5–10; of fiscal power 18; of governance authority 18; of power 6; tax-sharing system 12; tradition of 18
central-local relationship 3–5, 10
Central Organization Department 7
central personnel management 7
Charnes, A. 128
China: administrative laws in 61; central-local relationship 4; decision-maker 21; Economic Stimulus Program 37; fiscal decentralization strategy 3; governance goals 19; governance system 17; government reforms 54–60; "Indianization" of 60; institutional change 33; inter-provincial cooperation 65; market-oriented reforms 2; petitioning system 80; point-to-surface process 4; policy-makers 78; political development 29; political economy 33; political evolution for 77; political landscape 22; political stability 2; political system 3; proud transcript of 157; public administration 54; public policies 4; rural social pension insurance system 15; socialist political system 65; technological governance 25; unified state structure 5
China Agricultural University 159
China Internet Network Information Center 73
China National Knowledge Infrastructure (CNKI) 29
China Science and Technology Commissioner System 159
China's government reforms: complex adjustment process 63–67; five-yearly governmental reform 66; goals and realities 60–63; institutional reforms **58–59**; opening-up concludes 66; Western-centralism 60; western public administration 54–60
China's Internet era: authoritarian state 74; political legitimacy 78–79
Chinese Academic Community: adaptive governance 33–34; China, critics in 30–32; good governance 30–32; interactive governance 32–33; multi-level governance 32–33
Chinese bureaucratic cultures 57
Chinese Dream 34
Chinese experimentalism 15
Chinese governance: central government 1; challenges and trend of 24–26; characteristics of 16; experience of 16–17; extra-budgetary fiscal revenue **13**; governance rectification 17–20; governance structure 1; inclusive system 20–23; local governments 1; theoretical analysis 2
Chinese model 3
Christianity 60
The Civic Culture (Almond and Verba) 64
civil service 102
civil society 31, 32, 76
Clark, K. B. 99
The Clash of Civilizations (Huntington) 64
classified pilot 15
CNKI *see* China National Knowledge Infrastructure (CNKI)
co-evolutionary process 49
co-governance 17, 33
commercial areas 13
Communist Party of China 18, 76, 77; China's socialist path 34; leaders, role of 66; legitimacy of 76; responsibility, development 49; Socialist Education Campaign 49; state governance 21
competitive electoral system 78
competitive land management 13
complex adjustment process 63–67

complex theoretical system 4
"Comprehensive Petitioning Index" 81
computer technology 56
construction sector 38
consultative authoritarianism 1, 78
"contingent decision-making" 18
control variable screening 102–103
Cooper, R. B. 99
corruption, freedom from 75, 141, 143
Council issues Commands of the State Council (CSC) 61, 62
cross-sectional data analysis 54, 77, 126, 132
crowding-out effect 143
CSC *see* Council issues Commands of the State Council (CSC)
CSSCI (Chinese Social Sciences Citation Index) database 32
cultural background 64, 65
Cultural Revolution 2, 6
current political system reform 6
Cutler, Adele 102

Dahl, Robert 64
Data Envelopment Analysis (DEA) method 126, 128, 135
data unbalance assessment 103–106
DEA-Tobit method 127, 130, 137
De Borger, B. 128
decentralization 4, 17, 19; of authorities 61; of central government 6; central government's risk 17; of economic power 6; of governance authority 21; of personnel appointments 6; of power 6
decentralized authoritarianism 1, 3
decision-making ability 86
decision-making power 3, 15
decision-making unit (DMU) 128
democracy 22, 78, 103, **115**; development 14; durability of 134; indicator 133; institutional variables 132; meritocracy 53; public sector efficiency 137–138, **139–140**
democratic centralism 21, 22
democratic political system 137
democratization 76, 84; third wave of 22
De Montesquieu, C. 64
Denhardt, Janet 55, 57
Denhardt, Robert 55
dependent variables 101–102
descriptive statistics **134–135**
developed countries 53, 135; experience of 55; high input and even higher output 127
developing countries 53; economic growth of 29; low input and medium output 127; NPM reform 56; technical and economic needs 41
developmental state theory 25
deviant case 79
diachronic perspective 4
discretionary power 41
discrimination 75
diverse case 79
DMU *see* decision-making unit (DMU)

East Asia and Pacific regions 135
Eastern Europe 2
economic development 3, 11, 24, 25, 40
economic growth 2, 3, 11, 131
economic management power 10
economic performance 78
economic power 4
Economic Stimulus Program 37
Edelenbos, Jurian 33
education areas 13
e-government 73, 78, 79, 83; Zhejiang Province 83
Egypt 22
"the Eighteenth Brumaire of Louis Bonaparte" (Max) 97
engineering constructions 38–39
Enterprise Government theory 57
enthusiasm 11, 20
entrepreneur government theory 53
environmental governance 33
environmental pollution 35
environment protection output 131
EU Cohesion Policy 32
Europe 32
European debt crisis 55
Executive Commands of China's State Council 61
expenditure 11

extra-budgetary fiscal revenue 13, **13**
extreme case 79

false innovation 22
Farrell, M. J. 128
FDH *see* Free Disposable Hull (FDH)
Feasible Generalized Least Squared (FGLS) 107, 109
Fernandes, S. 131
FGLS *see* Feasible Generalized Least Squared (FGLS)
financial performance 18
fiscal decentralization system 11, 20; combination of 10–14; first phase, 1980 to 1993 10–11; gradual decentralization 10; second phase, 1994 to the present 11
fiscal transfer payments 3
five-yearly governmental reform 66
fixed effects model 107–108, 112, **113**
fixed income 11
flexible power structure 5
Flyvbjerg, B. 78
foreign governance 29
foreign reform 60
formal system 23
fragmented authoritarianism 3, 40
"fragmented authoritarianism 2.0" 78
Free Disposable Hull (FDH) 127, 128
Freedom House 133
French experience 66
Fukuyama, Francis 24

Gallagher, M. E. 77
General Plan for the Reform of Political System 6
Gerring, J. 78, 147n4
Gini-importance values 103
2008 global financial crisis 37
global governance 32
globalism/cosmopolitanism 56
globalization 56, 65
good governance 30–32
Google Scholar 29
governable democracy 21
governance/government 3; capacity 29; concept of 46; employees 67; failure 57; innovation, sustainability 25; investments 38; mechanism 21, 22; officials **44**; performance 54; policy implementations 35; political science 30; rectification 2, 17–20; reform 53; transparency 78; unbalanced income and expenditure 11
governing officials 3
government efficiency 78, 97; control variable screening 102–103; data unbalance assessment 103–106; dependent variables 101–102; executive authority 98; independent variables 101–102; machine learning 102–103; model construction 106–108; technological innovation 97
"government functional departments" 7
Gradstein, M. 147n3
grid-based governance model 22
Grimpe, C. 99
guerrilla policy-making style 33

Hassid, J. 77
Heilmann, S. 4, 33
Henderson, R. M. 99
heterogeneity 131
"hierarchical experimentation" concept 4
Hirschman, Albert O. 26
Hong, J. 76
Huai'an Sunshine Petitioning Online System 81–82, 92n1
Huhe, N. 77
Huntington, Samuel P. 64
Huntington, S. P. 60

"imitation of the West" 54
inclusive system 20–23
income distribution 131
independent variables 101–102
Indian Buddhism 60
industrial areas 13
inequality 80
inflation 131
informal systems 23
information censorship system 74, 77
information technology 74, 99
infrastructure investment 11
innovation diffusion theory 98
input-output ratio 128

institutional factors 137
institutional inclusion 2
institutional quality 141, 147n3; crowding-out effect 143; and public sector efficiency **144–145**; and regime durability **146**; role of 141–146
institutional reforms 54, **58–59,** 65
institutional variables 132
interactive governance 32–33
inter-government cooperation 39
international organizations 31
Internet 25, 73; censorship 76, 83; China's legitimacy 75–77; in China's political development 73; communication 76; consultative authoritarianism 83; cooperation 76; democratic nature 77; development of 75; governance strategies 77; information censorship system 74; and information technology 85; infrastructure 90; monitoring system 79; petition system 16; political influence 76; video monitoring system 90
Internet 2.0 25
"Internet+" national strategy 73
"Internet+ public service" 78
inter-provincial cooperation 65
"inverted U-curve" concept 101

Japan's Ministry of Trade and Industry 24
Jessop, B. 30
Johnson, Chalmers 24
joint-up government theory 53

Kerstens, K. 128
Kooiman, J. 33
Kornai, János 43
Kuznets, Simon 45, 101

labor productivity 3, 99
laissez-faire attitude 16
Lakoff, S. A. 75
late-developing countries 55
learning mechanism 15
Least Square Dummy Variables (LSDV) method 108
Lee, J. W. 132
Legal Office of the State Council 87
"*the Legislative Law*" 10
legislative power 7, 10
legitimacy crisis 74
Leo, Breiman 102
"letters and visits" system 79
liberal democracy 22
Lieberthal, K. 68
local governments 1; administrative authority 4; bureaucratic system 20; Chinese model 40; development of 10; enthusiasm of 6; extra-budgetary revenue 13; governance autonomy 6; "governing the people" 3; learning mechanism 15; regional characteristics 2; tax-sharing system 12; tournament system 3
localism 20
local land finance 13
local leaders: selection and appointment 7; self-governance ability 20
local leadership 6
local leading cadres 7
local legitimacy deficits 82
local self-governance 14–16, 15
local taxation scale 11
Locke, John 75
long-term governance goal 14
long-term institution 45
low-input-technology *158*
LSDV method *see* Least Square Dummy Variables (LSDV) method
Lynch, M. 77

machine learning 102–103
Mackinnon, R. 77
macroeconomic performance output 131
macro-governance: direction of 19; policies 18
macro-historical evolution 4
macroscopic control 12
Maerz, S. F. 83
market economy 12, 54
market-oriented reform process 2, 5, 6
market-preserving federalism 1
Marxism-Leninism principle 65
mathematical model 107

matrix governance structure 41, *42*, 43
maximum governance 42
Maximum Likelihood Estimator (MLE) 107
Max, Karl 97
medical areas 13
Mesthene, E. G. 75
micro-case analysis 4
Ministries and Committees (M&C) 62
Ministry of Human Resources and Social Security 15
Ministry of Land and Resources 12–13
MLE *see* Maximum Likelihood Estimator (MLE)
mobile information technology 25, 73
model construction 106–108; fixed effects model 107–108, 112; multiple linear regression 106–107, 109–111
moderate centralization 10–14
modern printing technology 99
modern technology 99
monitoring system 85–86
multi-collinearity test **108**
multi-level governance 32–33
multi-party election 75
multiple linear regression model 106–107, 109–111, **110–111**
multiple public administration theory 57

National Public Complaints 16
national tax revenue 11
NBER *see* US National Bureau of Economic Research (NBER)
New Public Management (NPM) 55
New Public Service theory 55, 57
non-government organizations (NGOs) 21, 32, 78
non-local principles 7
non-parametric DEA method 128
NPM *see* New Public Management (NPM)

oil crisis 1970s 54
old-style personal contribution system 15
Oliver, A. 83
OLPOS *see* orderly limited participation orientation strategy (OLPOS)
one-size-fits-all theory 53
online car-hailing service 79
online petitioning system 81
online public consultation systems 80
opening-up concludes 66
opportunity 6
orderly limited participation orientation strategy (OLPOS) 74, 79, 86–88
organic fertilizer 158
organizational innovation 99, 100
Orlikowski, W. J. 99
Osborne, D. 57
Ostrom, Elinor 55
overlapping administrative systems 41

Parsons, Talcott 20
Party's propaganda system 57
patent data 101
Patterns of Culture (Benedict) 64
People's Congress 86
Perry, E. J. 33
personnel management: pressure of 7; system 6
personnel power 6
"Petition Handling Satisfaction Index" 81
petitioning system 80, 89
phase—optimizing distribution 12
"pilot first and then promote" idea 14
pilot governance behavior 14
point-to-surface process 4
"police with science and technology" strategies 85
policy: distortions 20; experimentation 33–35; implementation system 47; learning 16; piloting 4; point-to-surface process 4; reproduction 16
Policy Analysis theory 57
policy-makers 67, 78
policy-makings 31, 41; phases of 33; process 33–35
political: corruption 103; decentralization 20; development 98; forum 82; freedom 78; imprisonment 103; influence

76; landscape 22; movement 6; opportunity structure 21, 73; participation system 31; resilience 2; rights 133; stability 2; system 3, 18; unity 1; visibility 54
Political Consultative Conference and Grassroots Democratic Elections 86
political legitimacy 77, 79–80; authoritarian regime 75; in China's internet era 78–79; and debates 76–77; in Internet era **91**; Internet politics impacts 75; source of 75–76
political power 4, 22; moderate decentralization of 5–10
Political Rights Indicator (PRI) 133
Polity IV Project 133
post-communist development 55
post-Mao leaders 33
poverty reduction 26, 46, 157, 158
power: abuse of 41; appointment and dismissal 6; balance of 12; central government 5; China's supreme organ 35; decentralization 6; decentralization of 3; distribution of 17, 18; operation of 6; political centralization 18; structure, transformation of 19
PRI *see* Political Rights Indicator (PRI)
"projects of improving human living conditions" 43
property rights protection 141, 147n3
Proposals Administration 16
PSE *see* public sector efficiency (PSE)
PSEOS *see* public service and efficiency-oriented strategy (PSEOS)
public: education output 131; governance authorities 4; health output 131; infrastructure output 131; investments 38, 132; management 64; opinions system 86, 87; policies 4; sector reform 47, 98; utility loan 31; values 21
public administration 14, 16, 18, 30, 53, 66; power distribution 21
Public Choice theory 57
public expenditure 127; environment protection output 131; input and output terms 130–132; macroeconomic performance output 131; public education output 131; public health output 131; public infrastructure output 131; scores and ranks of **154–156**
public-participation-oriented governance reform 23
public sector efficiency (PSE) 126, 127; cross-national 135–137; democracy 137–138; determinants of 132–135; input-oriented measures 127; institutional factors 137; institutional quality 141–146, **144–145**; non-parametric methods 128; public expenditure 130–132; regime durability 138–141, **142**; scores and ranks of 135, **136**
public service and efficiency-oriented strategy (PSEOS) 74, 79, 82–84
public services 3; apps for 83; economic development 98; efficiency of 54, 56; e-government 73, 92; quality of 55; social development 98

Quade, Edward 57

radical fiscal decentralization 11
random forest 102–103, **122–123**
"ratchet effect" 45
Rayp, G. 138
RDS *see* responsiveness-driven strategy (RDS)
recognition 15
regime durability 133, 138–141, **142, 146**
regional equilibrium pattern 11
Regulations on Rotations of Cadres 7
Reply Letters of the State Council (RLSC) 61, 62
residential areas 13
responsibility 3
responsiveness-driven strategy (RDS) 74, 79, 80–82
RLSC *see* Reply Letters of the State Council (RLSC)
robust test 115–116, **116**
Rosenbloom, David H. 55, 57
ruling party 77

rural development 157
rural social pension insurance system 15

Saaty, T. L. 67
"safety city" strategies 85
SCOS *see* social control orientation strategy (SCOS)
Seawright, J. 78
sectarianism 6
self-governance 26, 33
sensitive subject 77
separation idea 6
"servants-of-the-people" image 80
Seventh Plenary Session of the Twelfth Central Committee 6
SFA *see* Stochastic Frontier Approach (SFA)
simplicity 4
SIOG *see* special-issue-oriented governance (SIOG)
social constructivism 100, 112
social control orientation strategy (SCOS) 74, 79, 84–86
social governance 23
socialist democratic system 86
socialist political system 65
socialist system 60
social media 29, 76, 77
social security management 3, 85
social transformation 14
socio-economic divergence 131
socio-economic variables 141
socio-political environment 55
SOEs *see* state-owned enterprises (SOEs)
soft authoritarianism 3
Soviet Union 2
Spearman correlation coefficients 147n1
"special governance" 20
special-issue-oriented governance (SIOG): advantages and disadvantages 40–46; anti-corruption 35; characteristics of **48**; Chinese Academic Community 30–34; construction sector 38; in CPC documents **36**; cycle of *40*; developing countries 41; economic development 49; engineering constructions 38; governance, practice of 35–37; implementation process 37–40; mode and mechanism of 40; special operations team 39; in State Council Bulletin *37*; top-down policy process 39
Standing Committee of the National People's Congress 10
State Council: petition information system 16; *Report on the Work of the Government* 79
State Council Bulletin *37*
State Council Gazette 35, 46, 50n3
state-owned enterprises (SOEs) 10, 55, 63
state-owned land 13
Stochastic Frontier Approach (SFA) 127, 128
Stockmann, D. 77
Strayer, Joseph 65
substantive innovation 22
"Sunshine Letters and Visits" information system 16
"Sunshine Petition Online System" 79
"supervising two lower levels" system 5, 6
Sustainable Development Goals 55, 157

Tang, M. 77
Tang, W. 80
Taoism 60
tax decentralization 11
tax distribution system 11, 12
taxi-hailing service 87–88
tax income regulates 12
taxpayers **44**
tax-sharing system 10, 12, 55
technological determinism 98, 99, 109
technology innovation 97; application characteristics 99; democracy, high and low levels of 112–115; fixed effects model 112; government agencies 99; multiple linear regression 109–111; organizational innovation 99; political development 98; public sector reform 98; robust test 115–116; technological determinism 98

technology-organization-environment (TOE) 100
Thailand 22
theoretical systems 4
17th National Congress of the CPC 46
18th National Congress of the CPC 26
"*The 48th Statistical China's Report on Internet Development*" 73
Tianyan detection 79, 85–86
TOE *see* technology-organization-environment (TOE)
Tong, J. 77
top-down administrative system reform 22
top-down approach 14
top-down governance 33
top-down policy process 15, 39
top-level approach 15
top-level design 15, 16; combination of 14–16; public management 18
tournament system 3
transfer payment 11
transition process 5
Tsai, K. S. 33
typical case 78

ultra-nationalism 32
unbalanced income and expenditure 11
unemployment 131
United Nations Development Program 159
United Nations 2030 Sustainable Development Goals 159
United States 102
unity: destruction of 10; of responsibilities 7
universality 4
upper-level government 39
urban development 13
urbanization 138
U-shaped relation 97
US National Bureau of Economic Research (NBER) 101, 117
US Patent and Trademark Office (USPTO) 101
USPTO *see* US Patent and Trademark Office (USPTO)
US subprime mortgage crisis 55

value-added tax 11
Van De Sijpe, N. 138
"vanity or trophy projects" 90
Verba, Sidney 64
vertical management system 7, **8–9**
video conference system 99
VIF (Variance Inflation Factor) values 108

Wald test 147n5
Wall Street Journal 103
Wang, S. S. 76
Weel, B. 99
western administrative reform 63
Western-centralism 60
Western democracy 24
Western developed countries 54
western experience 54
western public administration 54; development of 54–60
western social-scientific methods 67
Western values 4
WIPO *see* World Intellectual Property Office (WIPO)
World Bank 31, 64, 65, 103, 117, 134
World Bank Open Data 131, 132
World Development Indicators 126
World Intellectual Property Office (WIPO) 101
World War II 54
Worldwide Governance Indicators 102

Zhejiang government service website 83–84
Zmud, R. W. 99
Zuo, L. 77

For Product Safety Concerns and Information please contact our EU
representative GPSR@taylorandfrancis.com
Taylor & Francis Verlag GmbH, Kaufingerstraße 24, 80331 München, Germany

www.ingramcontent.com/pod-product-compliance
Lightning Source LLC
Chambersburg PA
CBHW061739270326
41928CB00011B/2295

* 9 7 8 1 0 3 2 4 2 6 6 7 9 *